I have often heard that Chuck Byers is happiest when [illegible] not simply as a prolific wine writer and author, but also as a "terrific wine entertainer!"

This, indeed, is the Chuck I know, and aptly sums up the passion he shows for his work and how he makes everyone comfortable tasting, and talking about wine, whether they are connoisseurs or brand new to the experience.

Chuck's infectious enthusiasm in both his writing, and at the many wine tasting events that he hosts, has introduced countless Canadians to the fun of tasting wines at all price points. He is also a tireless promoter of homegrown products and for this, our industry is extremely grateful as he devotes so much time on television, radio and in the printed word extolling the strengths of our wine growing regions in Ontario and British Columbia.

Chuck is a wonderful teacher and a great friend to the wine industry.

Sincerely,

Don Triggs

Donald L. Triggs
President and Chief Executive Officer

"Peter Mielzynski Agencies has worked with Chuck for over 20 years promoting wines, spirits and beer. His knowledge, enthusiasim, and passion of our industry is second to none. PMA is proud to be involved with such a professional."

—Peter Mielzynski

"Ocala Winery Ltd. has long recognized the enthusiasm that Chuck Byers has felt for the Ontario wine industry and its products. We have been honoured by his support of the small, family run winery. His honest passion for wine is evident each time he raises his glass."

—Irwin L. Smith , Winemaker

"Chuck Byers is an honest and reputable person who has extreme passion, great experience and a vast understanding of the wine industry."

—Herbert Konzelmann, Wine Master, Konzelmann Estate Winery

Cheers!

"Chuck Byers writes in a nice easy conversational style and his enthusiasm about the Nova Scotian and Canadian Wine industries pours off each page."

--Hans Christian Jost, Jost Vineyards, Nova Scotia.

"I commend the author for acknowledging wine production from coast to coast to coast in Canada. Truly a Canadian approach, and I appreciate the inclusion."

—Winston Jennings, Manager - Notre Dame Winery, Durrell, NL.

"If we would rate wine writers like we do wine, Charles Byers would rate near the top in credibility, just ahead of his love and knowledge of wine."

—Alex Eberspaecher, International Wine Judge, Author, Wine and Travel Writer.

Rendezvous for Dinner

A Guide to Canadian Wine, Dining and Dessert

To a Great actor &
Thespian!
My very Best
[illegible]

Rendezvous for Dinner

A Guide to Canadian Wine, Dining and Dessert

by

Chuck Byers

with contributions from Tom Berki
and other chefs, bed and breakfasts,
wineries and restaurants

Cover design: de Sitter Publications
Cover photo: Permission to use photo granted by Pelee Island Winery
(www.peleeisland.com)
Content photography by Greg Muscat and Chuck Byers

Library and Archives Canada Cataloguing in Publication

Byers, C. A. (Charles Alexander)
Rendezvous for dinner: a guide to Canadian wine, dining and dessert / Charles Alexander Byers, Tom Berki.

ISBN 1-897160-18-6

1. Wine and wine making--Canada. 2. Cookery--Canada. 3. Wineries--Canada.
4. Bed and breakfast accommodations--Canada. I. Berki, Tom II. Title.

TP559.C3B83 2006 *641.2'2'0971*
C2005-907707-7

Table of Contents

News Flash

At the time of printing this book, Vincor International, which is mentioned throughout this book, was bought by Constellation Brands—a leading international producer and marketer of beverage alcohol brands located in Fairport, New York.

Mr. Donald Triggs, CEO and President of Vincor says that at this time the status quo will exist for the wineries owned by Vincor. It is safe to assume that the information concerning Vincor within this book will not change dramatically for some time to come. Future editions will of course include any and all changes.

—Chuck Byers

Dedication

The modern wine pioneers risked much to follow their dream. In doing so they fulfilled the dreams of thousands across this magnificent land called Canada. This book is dedicated to the following people who have contributed so much to both the national and international reputation of Canada's wine industry: Donald Ziraldo, Karl Kaiser, Donald Triggs, Allan Jackson, Harry McWatters, Hans Wilhelm Jost, Peter Mielzynski Senior, Roger Dial, Len Pennachetti and Herbert Konzelmann.

Special Thanks

I extend my sincerest thanks to Denis Drouin of Vignoble Cep D'Argent for his help with the wineries and food in the Province of Quebec; Winston Jennings, owner of Weil Winery/Notre Dame Wines for his assistance with Newfoundland's wines; Hans Christian Jost of Jost Vineyards in helping with Nova Scotia's wineries; and owners of the Victoria's Historic Inn and Carriage House, the Cryan Family, Steve, Sherrie and their parents Urbain and Carol, for their tireless efforts and hospitality in making our stay in Nova Scotia both enjoyable and successful.

Forward

I love wine—all aspects of it. I enjoy going into wine stores and looking at the rows upon rows of bottles awaiting selection. I love visiting wineries with their smell of fermentation, yeast and fruit. I love tasting all wines, homemade or commercial—good, bad or indifferent, because they all tell a story. Most of all I love seeing people enjoying wine—especially at that moment of anticipation as they open up a cherished bottle. Will it be good? Will it be past its prime? God let it be fine!

Wine picked me as one of its chroniclers for several reasons. I have an insatiable desire to be noticed (the ham in me!) More importantly, I am generally interested in history, geography, science, culture and people—all intrinsic in any study of wine.

Wine has been part of my life for some 30 years. Not one of those thirty has been a bore. There's always been something to learn each and every time I uncorked a bottle. The world of wine keeps on changing and evolving and each bottle presents the taster with a unique reality.

Some twenty years ago, it was quite easy to obtain a reasonably good bottle of wine without much risk or knowledge. Local liquor stores typically stocked French, Italian, and German wine. Since that time, many countries (mere fledglings 20 years ago) have come to challenge the most renowned of the 'old guard'. California was the spoiler in the 1970s and early 80s. Closely following California's success were Australia, Chile, South Africa, New Zealand, Argentina, Oregon and Washington. To add to the wealth (and confusion), older, established wine producing countries such as Austria, Spain, Italy, Portugal, Greece, Algeria, Hungry, Romania, Bulgaria and a host of peer countries (even the tiny Island of Malta) have updated their technical systems leading to clearly superior wines.

As the world of wine has gone through various incarnations in the past few years, so have I. While I 'cut my teeth' on French Bordeaux (I could repeat from memory all the five levels of the 'Classification of 1855 Bordeaux' in order of chateau placement) and Burgundy, my efforts became more focused on Ontario and now Canadian wines in general. My favourite wines in the 1980s were French Pauilliacs, St. Emilions and Burgundies. Now my favourites are wines from Ontario, Quebec, B.C. and Nova Scotia as well as fruit wines from Newfoundland, New Brunswick, Manitoba, Saskatchewan and Alberta.

Canada burst onto the world scene in the late 1980s and hasn't looked back. It clearly has rattled the 'nerves' of the world's wine producers with its many accomplishments since then. Canada as a wine producer wasn't supposed to make it. Around the world, the wines of Canada have clearly and consistently won major awards. Canada's climactic variations challenge the best viticulturists and winemakers to adapt methods and invent others in order to produce their wonderful nectar.

Work still has to be done at home in convincing a somewhat sceptical but warming public that Canada's wines are indeed among the best, anywhere. With the great work that is being done by V.Q.A., Wine Council of Ontario, British Colombia Wine Institute, the 'Cool Climate' programs at various universities and the wineries themselves, the greatness of Canada's wines will be assured in the future. With wine now being made in every province, it can be said that wine is achieving somewhat of a Canadian unity—achieving what many have failed to do. Rather than aiming to produce 'world quality' wines, the world will aim to produce 'Canadian quality' wines.

Acknowledgements

The following have been an invaluable inspiration, encouragement and aide to me in the writing of this book. I would like to thank them for their great assistance.

Fred/Sandy Archibald	Archibald Orchards/Estates Winery (see description for website).
Tony Aspler	Winewriter, Consultant and Author, www.tonyaspler.com
Bernie Hadley-Beauregard	Principal, Brandever Strategy Inc. www.brandever.com
Dan Carter	Executive Producer Programming, CHEX T.V. www.channel2.ca/dap1.htm
David Cryan Family	Victoria's Historic Inn B&B www.victoriashistoricinn.com
Sal D'Angelo	D'Angelo Vineyards Ontario/B.C. www.dangelowinery.com
Denis Drouin	Cep D'Argent Winery, Quebec www.cepdargent.com
Dominique/Cindy Duby	Wild Sweets www.dcduby.com
Alex Eberspaecher	Wine, Food and Travel Writer www.winecop.com
East of the City Magazine	Angie Cosette, Editor Amy West, Publication Editor Alicia Veloce, Assistant Editor www.durhamregion.com/dr/east/adinfo
Tino & Nick Fazio	Fazio's Restaurant, Oshawa, ON www.faziosrestaurant.ca
Gordon, Bonnie	Bonnie Gordon Cakes www.bonniegordoncakes.com
J L Groux	Stratus Vineyards, Niagara www.stratuswines.com
Jane Holland	Lewis Carroll Communications www.lewiscarrollcom.com
Alan Jackson	Co-founder, Jackson-Triggs Estates Winery www.jacksontriggswinery.com

Cathy Jacobs	V/P Marketing, Vincor Int'l. Cathy.Jacobs@Vincor.Ca
Hans Christian Jost	Jost Vineyards www.jostwine.com
Herbert Konzelmann	Konzelmann Estate Winery www.konzelmannwines.com
Barry A Katzman	President, Creekside Estates Winery www.creeksidewine.com
Peter Koscis	Owner/winemaker, Crown Bench Winery www.crownbenchestates.com
Paul Lizac	President/Winemaker Legends Estates Winery www.legendsestates.com
Angelo Pavan	Partner/winemaker Cave Spring Cellars www.cavespringcellars.com
Charles Pillitteri	Pillitteri Estates Winery www.pillitteri.com
Martin Polidano	Fazio's Ristorante www.faziosrestaurnant.ca
Jenn Stone	Jenn's Bon Bons, Toronto www.jsbonbons.com
Hanspeter Stutz	Domaine de Grand Pre www.grandprewines.com
James Le Fresne	Train Station Inn, Tatamagouche, N.S. www.trainstation.ns.ca
Todd McDonald	National Manager, PMA Canada www.pmacanada.com
Harry McWatters	Founder, Sumac Ridge Winery British Co lombia www.sumacridge.com
Peter D. Mielzynski	President, PMA Canada www.pmacanada.com
Liz O'Neill,	Executive Associate, Pelee Island Winerywww.peleeisland.com
Debi Pratt	Winery Public Relations, Inniskillin Winery www.inniskillin.com
Klaus Reif	Owner/winemaker Reif Estate Winery www.reifwinery.com
Greg Rist	Producer, Rogers Television www.grist@rci.rogers.com

Del Rollo	Manager of Hospitality Relations Jackson -Triggs, Niagara
John Rossignol	Rossignol Estate Winery www.rossignolwinery.com
Michael Semak	Photographer/Photojournalist (Internet search Semak: Meet the Artist)
Colin Sines	Director of Marketing, Vintage Inns www.vintageinns.com
Irwin Smith	Ocala Winery www.ocalawinery.com
Paul Speck	Henry of Pelham Estate Winery www.henryofpelham.com
Steven Simick	Manager, Rogers Community Television, Oshawa www.rogers.com
Donald Triggs	CEO/President Vincor International , Co-Founder Jackson -Triggs www.jacksontriggswinery.com
Diane Turner	Marketing Coordinator, Vintage -Inns www.vintageinns.com
Kevin Wagner	Cooking Solutions www.cooking-solutions.com
John and Virginia Weber	Orofino Winery, B.C. www.orofinovineyards.com
Margo Weir	Whitby Chamber of Commerce www.whitbychamber.org
Doug White	Bed and Breakfast Online Canada www.bbcanada.com
Jay Wright	President of Vincor Canada www.vincor.ca
Midge Wyse	Burrowing Owl Estate Winery www.bovwine.ca
Dennis Yurkiwsky	Chocolate Exquisite www.chocolateexquisite.ca
Donald Ziraldo	Co-Founder Inniskillin Winery www.inniskillin.com

Special thanks to:
The Chambers of Commerce Canada Wide

About the Book

In 1998, I began to see the value and potential of Canadian wine. Canada was beginning to move and gain momentum—especially with its fabulous ice wines and emerging white and red premium wines. At the time, there were about 60 wineries scattered in Nova Scotia, Ontario, Quebec and B.C. Today, Canada is a world leader in Cool Climate Technology and its wines are winning awards and recognition throughout the globe. The number of Canadian wineries is now almost 300—each making quality award winning wines. There is at least one winery in each of Canada's ten provinces.

In this book, I categorize some 250 wineries across Canada. I diligently emailed and called many of these wineries to verify addresses and contact information. I took the utmost care to double check all the facts and information. To all those individuals, wineries and hospitality centers that assisted me, a very big thanks to you.

One note about the wineries, many of the wineries listed are grape based wineries. However, there are a large number that produce either just fruit wines or a combination thereof. The wineries that produce fruit wines are serious wineries creating excellent products that are unique in their own right.

Some 50 wineries from this list are matched with original recipes. The majority are provided by Tom Berki, owner of the Rendezvous Bistro, in Ajax Ontario. In addition, I personally selected contributions from wineries, chefs, restaurants and Bed & Breakfasts throughout Canada.

In the back of this book there are two winery lists. One is as comprehensive contact list of most wineries in Canada arranged alphabetically, regionally and provincially. The second list describes the wineries used in combinations with the various recipes. These wineries (and their websites) are also arranged alphabetically, regionally and provincially. The wineries described in detail are printed in *italics* in the master list.

Readers who enjoy sweets will enjoy the section about wine, dessert and chocolate. In addition, 'wine tips' have been specifically included to assist with the enjoyment of wine with various food themes as well as on its own.

Many wineries offer fantastic tours of their establishments, attracting tourists from around the world. While visiting wineries across Canada, I had the opportunity to lodge at some of the finest Bed and Breakfasts. Of course, there are many reputable B&B's. In this book, I list 50 B&B's within reasonable distance of wineries. My selections are based on personal appeal, closeness to the wineries, historical significance and other interesting tidbits that I encountered during my cross-country tour.

I am a history buff. Knowing history some how brings me closer to the subject that I am studying. While on the road, I discovered countless historical gems about Canadian wineries and wine. After reading the brief historical section about our wineries, I am sure that you will be spurred on to find out more.

Touring the industry has been a great journey and learning experience. The acknowledgement section includes people who have taught me through their work and example. I thank them with great humbleness and humility.

I hope that you will be encouraged to learn more about this astounding and forever amazing beverage called Canadian Wine.

Canadian Cuisine

I love to eat and the fact that I've got an 'iron stomach' means that I can basically eat what I want, when I want. Consuming doesn't make me a gourmet chef, but it does allow me to experiment with wine and food.

Born on the Island of Malta does have its merits. Malta's food is varied and reflects the tastes of many eastern and western cultures. When I came to Canada, the hotdog, hamburger and even bacon and eggs were as alien to me as rabbit stew, fried Lampuka and Timpana would be to most Canadians. I adjusted and adapted my tastes as my exposure grew. I have experienced 'Canadianized' foods from many cultures: Chinese, Lebanese, Greek, Italian, South American, Japanese, Jordanian, Egyptian, Slavic, Polish, Indian, Punjabi, Caribbean and a host of other countries both familiar and exotic. Canada is indeed a melting pot!

In writing this book, I draw upon my exposure to a variety of foods and different ways of preparing dishes. In this edition, I include dishes that reflect Canada's food heritage.

Canada is a melting pot of culture and cuisine. Every province from Newfoundland to British Colombia has its unique food contributions from people who chose to settle there.

While this book focuses on wine, without food to provide a complimentary backdrop, wine cannot fulfill its destiny. To our senses, food fulfills wine and wine fulfills food. It is a symbiotic relationship—a perfect marriage. I hope you enjoy our selections.

—Chuck Byers

A BRIEF HISTORY OF WINEMAKING IN CANADA

Some Ancient History

Canadian wine consumers should read about the exploits of Leif Ericson. After landing at Lance aux Meadows in Newfoundland, he (or his men) found grape vines (or some reasonable facsimile, such as Blueberries). From the grapes, they made wine and decided to call the area Vineland. It was, however, the clergy who, needing wine in order to celebrate mass, first officially made wine in Canada. The Jesuits found a very harsh environment but they were delighted to find wild grapes (probably a species of Vitis riparia)[1] that they could use to make wine. It was not the best wine by any standards, being harshly acidic and low in alcohol, but it fulfilled their needs. Planting grapevines and winemaking goes back to as far as the sixteenth century in The Province of Quebec. Planting vines is recorded in early seventeen century in Nova Scotia (although real efforts did not take place there until early in the twentieth century).

Attempts were made to grow European varieties, but the European varieties could not withstand the weather and diseases. Native grapes were obviously resistant or even immune to the harsh conditions. Some very famous people both in

Canada and the United States attempted to grow European vines. Lord Delaware (1619), Lord Baltimore (1662), William Penn (1683) and even Thomas Jefferson (1770). All failed!

There was a silver lining to this failure, however. It seems that some of the European or Vitis vinifera vines that were planted survived long enough to cross-pollinate with native species. Out of this union came newer hybrids that had the characteristics of both—higher sugar levels, resistance to local diseases and ability to withstand colder temperatures.

A retired soldier, John Schiller, began cultivating wild vines in a plot near Cooksville, Ontario around 1811. He later expanded to the growing of American hybrids that he purchased from settlers from the United States. Schiller became so successful that he began selling his surplus.

His property was later sold to Justin de Courtney who established a winery that went on to gain international recognition at the Paris Exposition of 1867. In 1873, George Barnes, a relative of a vintner and shipper called Porter Adams, founded a winery near St. Catherines, Ontario. A year later, T.G. Bright founded his winery. By the year 1900, there were some 5,000 acres of vines under cultivation in the Niagara Peninsula.

British Colombia vineyards got their start around the mid-1800s when missionaries planted vines a few miles south of Kelowna. This led to further plantings and winery openings in the late nineteenth century. However, the first commercial thrust in B.C. was not until the late 1920s and early 30s when the Calowna Wines were established.

There was a significant event that encouraged the introduction of cultivable grape vines to Canada. This was the devastating 'Phylloxera'[2] epidemic during the latter half of the nineteenth century, which almost destroyed all of Europe's vineyards. Grafting[3] European vine cuttings to American rootstocks proved the best way to battle this pest, although other resistant hybrids, some of which are known today, were developed by crossing strains of vinifera vines with American species. The result was the creation of some well-known grape varieties such as Baco Noir, Marechal Foch, Villard-Noir, Seyval Blanc, Chelois and Vidal Blanc.
Ironically, the problems in Europe made it possible for quality grapes to be grown on Canadian soil.

The Emergence of a New Industry

Canadians became known as major consumers of wine after Prohibition in the 1930s. Attempts to control the drinking habits of Canadians led to the emergence of the L.C.B.O. in Ontario (1928) and the 'Wine Standards Committee'.

The large wineries began investigating the suitability of growing hybrid grapes in Ontario. In 1946, one shipment consisted of about 200 grape varieties including some vinifera species.

In an experiment, large parts of Niagara were uprooted (Labrusca)[4] and replanted with various French hybrids such as Baco Noir, Seyval Blanc, de Chaunac and Marachal Foch. In 1955, there were plantings of Pinot Noir and Chardonnay, which resulted in varietal wines that were good enough to be encouraging for future consideration.

The French hybrids gave Ontario (and thus Canada) a chance to make wines of reasonable quality. In British Colombia, Andrew Peller founded Andres Wines (1961) and went on to produce some 'catchy' wines by the name of Cold Duck and Hoctaler in the 1970s. Also in 1961, Mission Hill Winery was founded in B.C. Back in Ontario in 1973, The Podamer Champagne Company (later purchased by Magnotta Winery) was making sparkling wines from French hybrids.

The Era of Boutique Wineries—The Age of Vinifera Begins!

Up until the 1970s, Canadian wine was for the most part made cheaply, ameliorated (watered down) and subsidized by the government. Storm clouds on the horizon in the form of the North American Free Trade Agreement and the future rescinding of the subsidy gave the Canadian wine trade something to worry about. The industry needed to modernize to provide quality wines that would compete with those of the United States (California) and the rest of the world. The answer came from what was to become a 'catch phrase'—Boutique Wineries. In 1975, two men changed the whole look of the Canadian wine industry.

After securing the first winery license since the 1930s, Donald Ziraldo (B.Sc. Agriculture, University of Guelph) and Karl Kaiser (Chemist, Brock University) promptly founded Inniskillin Winery. They set out to make quality wines using French hybrid and vinifera grapes. In 1975, Inniskillin Winery opened its doors. It was a small operation that produced lower volume but very high quality wine. The term 'Boutique Winery' stuck with the founders, but is now joined by many wine producers such as Chateau des Charmes, Cave Spring Cellars,

Konzelmann Estates, Hillebrand[5] and Reif Estates to name a few. B.C.'s first boutique winery, Claremont, was founded in 1979 and was later joined by Sumac Ridge, owned by Harry McWatters, who is still going strong.

Initially, the wineries produced quality wines made from French hybrids and also from 100% vinifera vines. Then, as the technology grew and clones[6] developed, vinifera vines began to replace the hybrids. Presently, Vitis vinifera vines have replaced most of the French hybrid vineyards of Ontario. British Colombia, having started somewhat later than Ontario, has been making 100% vinifera wines, while Quebec and Nova Scotia both leaned to use mostly hybrids with some vinifera vines.

Canadian Wines Rise to Prominence

The world community started paying attention to Canadian wines in the mid-1980s. As far back as 1982, a Burgundian shipper by the name of Chauvenet ordered about 650 cases of 1980 Inniskillin Marechal Foch, causing quite a stir at the time.[7] The real excitement, however, started in 1991, when an Inniskillin 1989 Vidal Icewine won a gold medal at Vinexpo in Bordeaux, France. This was akin to Dr. Roger Bannister's[8] legendary record of running a mile under four minutes in the 1950s. Canadian wineries reached a standard that demanded serious attention. Skeptics and critics remained stubborn, but they were soon silenced. Competition after competition, from one country to the next, Canada's wine producing provinces consistently brought home more than one top award.

Soon, fraudulent imitations of Canadian Icewine surfaced from the Orient. A syrupy wine, which is a mere shadow of the gold medal Icewine, was bottled and labeled to appear as Canadian Icewine. Canadian wineries took, and are taking, drastic action to counteract this threat.[9] On the bright side, reproductions are a sure sign of success!

Perhaps it is not surprising that the Canadian consumer has been the hardest to convince about the quality of their nation's wines. Canadians experience of wine still lingers in the yesteryear when quality was debatable and fine wines from other countries were readily available. Canadians are slowly warming to their wines. Developing a market and changing attitudes and opinions is a very difficult task. What was needed was an assurance of quality. As we shall see, this came into being in a very unique way.

The Founding of the Vintners Quality Alliance

As mentioned previously, in 1982 an agreement occurred between a Burgundian shipper named Chauvenet and Inniskillin Winery for the sale of 650 cases of 1980 Marechal Foch. However, the sale did not conform to the French's 'appellation of origin'[10] regulations, which have to be followed by any country exporting wine to France. The sale was cancelled. This prompted a movement (which Mr. Ziraldo was involved in) to forge ahead with Ontario's (and later B.C.'s) answer to the 'appellation system' by creating the Vintners Quality Alliance (V.Q.A.), an independent body responsible for introducing and maintaining standards and appellations adopted by members of the Ontario wine industry.[11]

The V.Q.A. itself is divided in several levels. The first and most basic is the 'Provincial Designation,' meaning that 100% of the wine must be made from grapes grown within that province. The next level up is called 'Designated Viticultural Areas,' for example, Niagara Peninsula, Lake Erie North Shore or Pelee Island. The wine from this designation must be made from 100% Ontario grapes with 85% of the product from one of the designated areas above. The final level is the 'Estate Bottled' and/or 'Vineyard Designations' where the wines must be made from 100% Ontario grapes grown 100% within the estate or vineyard named. The vineyard must also be within one of the specific designated regions.

On December 6, 2005, V.Q.A. was upgraded to include 12 new sub-appellations (districts) within the Niagara Peninsula Geographic Designation. The Niagara Peninsula Geographic Designation was divided into two broad sub-appellations: Niagara-on-the Lake and Niagara Escarpment. The Niagara-on-the-Lake and Niagara Escarpment were broken down into 10 additional sub-appellations. These sub-appellations are unique in their soil, climate and topography and are thus so reflected in wines that are produced within them. The new sub-appellations are: Niagara Lakeshore, Niagara River, Four Mile Creek, St. David's Bench, Creek Shores, Lincoln LakeShore, Beamsville Bench, Twenty Mile Bench, Short Hills Bench, Vinemount Bench. In order to have the above appellation(s) on the bottle label(s) all wines must be made from grapes grown 100% within the appellation(s).

The Vintners Quality Alliance covered all aspects of growing grapes and making wine. Grape types, labels, minimum sugar levels, packaging, panel tastings and evaluations, special designations, and awards—all are detailed by the V.Q.A.

A similar transformation happened in British Colombia in 1990 with four Designated Viticultural Areas being named: The Okanagan Valley, Similkameen Valley, Fraser Valley and Vancouver Island. Though British Colombia was influenced by Ontario's V.Q.A., there are rules that are specific and unique to each provincial region. With this new instrument of quality assurance and enforceable standards, the stage was set for movement both at home and abroad.

Canada Begins to Shine

There were key moves in the industry that assured the public of the quality of Canadian wines. Acclaimed wine writer, wine consultant, and wine judge, Tony Aspler founded the Ontario Wine Awards in 1995. His wish was to have a venue for V.Q.A. to recognize and promote top Ontario wineries and their wines. Enlisting the aid of the Ontario Wine Industry, he succeeded in launching the annual Awards show.

In 1997, for the first time, students could enroll in university degree and research programs at Brock University's Cool Climate Oenology and Viticulture Institute and University of B.C.'s wine research program and winemaking programs at Niagara College (Ontario) and Okanagan University College (B.C.).

The Wine Council of Ontario in partnership with the provincial government and the Ontario wine industry launched a marketing strategy that looked far into the future. The Canadian Vintners Association was joined by the Ontario Wine Council and the British Colombia Wine Institute in 1999, thus forming a national body.

In 2000, the voluntary organization, V.Q.A., became law—governing all wineries within the V.Q.A. membership, and regulating the use of terms and designations such as 'Icewine,' and how products are made. This meant that the V.Q.A. had clout which it could use to deter and reprimand rule breakers. Public acceptance of the V.Q.A. is certainly evidence that Canadians recognize and trust the quality of Canadian wines.

Another industry law that inspired confidence was the enactment of the Wine Content Act of Ontario in 2001. It regulates winemaking and labeling.

All of this progress toward ensuring the highest quality and standards has placed Canada as a premium wine producer at all levels of world competition. Foreign investors and very smart Canadian marketers are capitalizing on the wine industry's long road to success.

The Rise of Vincor: Canada's Wine Ventures Out!

Ziraldo, McWatters, Pennachetti, Mielzynski, Pillitteri, and Jost have become known as legendary pioneers of the Canadian wine industry. Although Donald Triggs, a marketer, arrived on the scene shortly after this group, his influence on Canadian wine certainly affords him a special place in our history.

Born on a cattle ranch in Manitoba, Donald was very close to 'mother nature' and his family. After graduated from the University of Manitoba with a B.Sc. in agriculture and received his MBA from the University of Western Ontario, he worked for Colgate-Palmolive, ran the global horticultural business for Fisons, PLC and was President of the American Wine Group.

Fate played a part when Labatt's invited a Ph.D. and wine lover chemist by the name of Allan Jackson to improve the quality of their Canadian wines (keep in mind what the underlying situation in the industry was like at that time).[12] Allan met Donald and they fast became good friends.

In 1989, they bought out Labatt's Canadian interests and formed Cartier Wines and Beverages. After several acquisitions and mergers (Inniskillin in 1992 and Brights in 1993), Vincor International Inc. with Triggs as President and CEO was created the same year. Also in 1993, Triggs and Jackson co-founded Jackson-Triggs Vintners.[13] However, their efforts did not end there!

Vincor quickly became the fourth largest wine producer in North America by acquiring holdings throughout Canada, Australia, New Zealand, South Africa, the United Kingdom and the United States.[14] Partnerships with European wine companies were formed that developed ambitious projects such as 'Le Clos Jordan', a new winery, located on the Niagara Bench, producing premium Pinot Noir and Chardonnay. The partnership between Vincor and Boisset Pere et fils of Burgundy set out to develop an ultra premium wine venture with a 'see through' winery building designed by world famous architect, Frank Gehry.[15]

Traveling some 300,000+ miles every year, Triggs promoted Canadian wines and ensured that it remained competitive in a very competitive market. Very interested in the future of wine research in Canada, he became an important contributor to Brock University's Cool Climate Programs.

Ontario's (Canada's) Wine Plan in Place: 'Poised for Greatness'

The players for the successful promotion of Canadian wines whether from British Colombia, Ontario, Nova Scotia and Quebec were in place and poised for action. In 2000, the Wine Council of Ontario released its 'Wines of Ontario: Sales and Marketing Plan', which included a strategic framework for the Ontario Wine Industry. A twenty-year action plan was developed that included everything from agro tourism, consumer education and branding to premium/ultra-premium wine, licensee education and target markets. The focal point of the plan is to take an $860 million industry and make it a 2.7 billion industry by 2020.[16]

In the 2004 Annual V.Q.A. report, Len Pennachetti, President, Cave Spring Cellars and President/Chairperson of the V.Q.A. Ontario expressed 'another successful year' of the V.Q.A. as Ontario's wine authority. Sales volume was up 1% over the previous year. He went on to mention that work would go on to identify sub-appellations within the Niagara Peninsula and Lake Erie North Shore.[17]

It was also mentioned that V.Q.A. Ontario would be working on improved national and international recognition for the V.Q.A. wine standard. Here, Mr. Pennachetti touched on an Agreement on Wine and Spirits between the Government of Canada and the European Commission for better access of Canadian V.Q.A. wines to European markets.[18]

Canada's Wine Regions: Continuous Development towards Continuous Success

History shows that what goes around usually comes around. The Canadian wine history started with Europeans, namely the French, trying to maintain a piece of their civilization by growing vines in a hostile and desolate wilderness. Imagine the hard work and disappointment faced by those who struggled to cultivate the first viniferas that were doomed to die of disease. Imagine their elation at finding some accidental hybrids between the native and viniferas. Imagine what they would think about the strides that the Canadian wine industry has made in the three hundred years that have gone by since.

The industry is still moving forward. Old appellations are now being revised. New wine regions such as those of Prince Edward County and Durham Region in Ontario are being developed and technologies being derived to assist them. Quebec wineries are increasing in number and fine tuning their quality. Nova Scotia is now a serious contender producing quality wines. New Brunswick and Newfoundland also make wine that is unique to their region. Prince Edward Island has a truly distinctive industry given that there is only one winery, which has grapes grown within glass solariums. As mentioned previously, there are now wineries in every Canadian Province.[19]

Success doesn't happen overnight. It takes a visionary to turn land into a vineyard. It takes a visionary to build a world class, wine producing system. It takes great risks and many sleepless nights. We owe a vote of thanks to Ziraldo, Jost, Stutz, Dial, McWatter, Pavan, Pennachetti, Pillitteri, Kaiser, Konzelmann, Reif, Bosc, Pohorly, Negri, Smith, Triggs and too many others to mention. The story of Canada's wines is just beginning.

CANADA'S WINES

You may be surprised by the diversity of Canadian wines. A brief synopsis of Canadian wine will help as guide to the choices.

Dessert Wines

Dessert wines lead the pack. Why? Inniskillin 1989 Vidal Icewine is the answer. Since the Vin Expo in 1991, Canada's wine industry became synonymous with its dessert wines because of Icewines. These luscious wines have a unique sweetness that is neither overpowering nor cloying. There is major difference between the harmonic base of true Icewine (where sweet, bitter, salt and acid tastes combine in perfect union) and that of others where sweet syrup is the dominant flavour.

Icewines are expensive because of the unique process. For instance:

- A plot of land has to be selected especially for the icewine grapes. The grapes must also be protected from birds etc. by netting.
- The grapes used must be from specific types required by the V.Q.A. standards (usually, Riesling, Vidal, Gewurztraminer, Cabernet Franc).
- Grape sugar levels must be at a minimum 32° Brix.[20]
- Three to five days of continuous temperatures of at least -7°C (preferably

-10°C or more) is needed for harvesting to begin.

- The grapes must be harvested manually (usually at night to ensure maximum cold).
- Ice crystals within the grapes must be separated from the rest of the grape.
- The crushing/pressing must take place on the spot, immediately after the harvest in the same viticultural area where the grapes were grown.
- Special yeasts tolerant of the high sugar concentrations are needed for adequate fermentation.
- The amount of wine produced is very low compared to that of regular wine.

So why make it? The resulting luscious liquid is like no other wine. A taste of V.Q.A. Icewine is a journey into olfactory heaven![21]

Other Canadian dessert wines that are held in high acclaim are Late Harvest Wine, Select Late Harvest Wine, Special Select Late Harvest Wine and many of Canada's top fruit wines. There are also some supplies of Vin de Cure.[22] Canada also produces fortified wines also such as Port Style and Sherry Style wine.

White Table Wine

Eons ago (or what seems to be a long time ago), Canadian white table wine was watered down, sugar coated and not very good. Several events led to greatly improved taste and quality.

The NAFTA (North American Free Trade Agreement) between the United States, Mexico and Canada and GATT (General Agreement on Tariffs and Trade), meant that the Canadian wine industry had to either improve its wine and make it competitive or close down.[23]

Many winemakers from all over the world, including Italy, Germany and France, saw the potential for producing quality wine grapes in Canada.

Technology was moving ahead with new ideas and new viticultural techniques such as special clones of grape varieties and growing methods.

Ideas for Agro-Tourism[24] within Ontario and then British Colombia spurred on the escalation of winemaking and the wine trade in general.

The establishment of the V.Q.A. set the rules and regulation for quality winemaking.

New interest and success in vinifying French hybrid white grapes, for instance, Vidal and Seyval Blanc encouraged attempts at vinifera species such as

Chardonnay, Riesling and Gamay Noir which furthered the movement to other grape varieties including Pinot Noir, Cabernet and Zweigelt.

Presently, the white wines of Canada come in a multitude of styles and varieties—each with its own distinctive regional characteristic and each with tremendous potential for excellence. The tastes range from the full bodied butterscotch and vanilla Barrel Fermented Chardonnay to the superbly herbaceous Sauvignon Blanc to the pleasant acidity of Riesling or Pinot Gris. All special! All great!

Red Wines

Red wines are latecomers to the field of excellence mainly because the process of making red wine is more involved than making white wine. Red wine usually goes through a second fermentation called Malolactic Fermentation.[25] Care must be taken also not to over filter wines (passing wine through a filter or several filters to remove debris, etc.), since red wine reacts to filtration by losing colour and taste if filtration is overused. Some wineries produce premium wines that are not filtered at all. Usually, unfiltered or lightly filtered wines can age for much longer periods of time than their filtered counterparts, which are usually made for early drinking. Canada, again, had success with such French hybrids as Marechal Foch, De Chaunac and Baco Noir. They age very well to an almost Burgundian style. This encouraged winemakers to move on to the Cabernets, Merlots and Pinot Noirs—all of which have reached great success. Special clones conducive to each region's weather were selected and special cultivation techniques used. The result has been the production of enormously successful wines that are similar in style to the best reds anywhere, including Bordeaux and Burgundy. Attempts are also being made to grow Syrah (Shiraz) and Sangiovese. Once again, time and weather will tell.

However, don't completely discount the French hybrids. While vinifera seems to be the king, many wineries are making fantastic Baco Noir (Henry of Pelham) as well as ultra superb Marechal Foch (Malivoire, Jost, Grand Pre).

Sparkling Wines

Canadian sparkling wines are now coming of age. For years, poorly made sparkling wines were made under names such as Canadian Champagne giving serious sparkling wines a very hard hill to climb. While it is illegal to use the term Champagne on the labels of anything other than actual Champagne Bottles,[26] many top Canadian sparkling wines are using the exact process known as the Methode Champenoise (of Champagne Method) for making it. The process is thus:

- Grapes are chosen and fermented normally.
- The wine is bottled and then yeast is added and sealed.
- The yeast ferments within the bottle producing Carbon Dioxide Gas.
- The bottles are placed 'top slanting downward' in a rack. This encourages the waste material of fermentation to settle near the cork section.
- The bottles are turned one-quarter turn per day either by machine or hand called 'Riddling' or 'Reumage' in French.
- After a period of time (1 year minimum), the dead yeast cells other debris are removed from the bottle. The French call it 'Degorgement'. The top of the bottle is frozen thus forming an icecap where the material to be removed is. The bottle top is then removed and pressure forces out the debris along with some wine.
- The bottle is then refilled with the same wine, a measure of liqueur.[27] The French call this 'Dosage'. The percentage of sweetness can increase from the one percent solution for a brut or dry sparkling wine to as much as 10 percent or more for a sweet sparkling wine.

After a period of rest, the bottles are sold.

Methode Champenoise (Champagne Method) or Traditional Method or Classic Method produces bubbles that are always smaller and longer lasting than other sparkling winemaking methods. There are two other techniques in use. The Charmat Method of making sparkling uses large pressurized steel tanks for secondary fermentation. The wine is then filtered and bottled. This is a cheaper method of making sparkling wine but usually does not result in the same high quality taste or small bubble size. The Transfer Method uses the bottle as the secondary fermentation, after which it is disgorged into pressurized tanks, filtered and replaced in the bottle. This method is not used in Canada because the Charmat Method is cheaper and the Traditional (Classical, Champagne) Method is more widely recognized and accepted.

Canadian sparkling wine is now among the best in its class. And, fortunately for us, it is excellent for a wide variety of foods.

Tasting Canadian Sparkling Wine

I try to avoid getting caught up in rules. When it comes to tasting wine, I have no rules, only suggestions. Here are a few tips.

1. Place your bottle of wine in a mixture of ½ ice and ½ water for about 15 to 25 minutes.
2. When it reaches the desired temperature of about 10°C (50° F), wrap the bottle in a towel. Take off the cage wire. Hold the neck of the bottle with your thumb and/or towel on the cork. Twist the bottom of the bottle to the right with your free hand.[28] Remember to hold the cork steady and point it away from people and other breakable bottles of wine.
3. Pour wine into a glass about ½ to ¾ full. Use a flute glass, it will allow you to see the bubbles and it keeps them from dissipate quickly. Wide-rimmed glasses normally associated with champagne are neither good for champagne nor Canadian sparkling wine.
4. Sip it alone, perhaps with some friends, but absolutely try it with a host of foods—love those oysters!

> To shuck or not to shuck? A question to compare. No oyster wishes to be there. Splattered with lemon or balsamic, it wonders 'Why all the haste?' But with texture so silky and taste so sublime, it realizes its fate was not to be part of my rhyme!

FOOD AND WINE: IT'S A MATTER OF TASTE

Facts about Tasting

Rest assured; we use the same senses when we drink wine as we do when we eat food. Our first sense involves ***sight***—if it looks good, we expect it should taste good. But, we've all been fooled before. That's why we can *smell*—if it smells horrid no matter how good it looks, we should pass. Unfortunately, curiosity has driven us down that familiar road too. That is why we can taste—to satisfy our curiosity. When imbibe liquids, even orange juice, we should swirl the liquid so it mixes with the air to release the aroma. But here is where it gets complicated—taste and smell are very closely connected. (There's a reason why dogs sniff with their mouths open!)

Smell or aroma alerts our sensory receptors to the possibilities of pleasure or pain. When we taste something the experience is weighed against our initial expectations based on smell. If we expected a dish to taste fantastic (because it smells great) but it only tastes 'ok, then you would be very disappointed. If a dish smells 'ok' and it tastes 'ok', you would not be disappointed. The larger the gap between our expectations and experiences, the greater our elation or disappointment. How something smells and tastes gives balance to the whole process.

Taste involves sweetness (tip of tongue), acid (sides of tongue) and bitterness (back of tongue). When we drink or chew, the food is automatically rolled in the mouth. This allows receptors in all areas of the tongue to send pertinent information to the brain as to the balance and mouth feel of the item being consumed. The next sensory appreciation is the *swallowing* of the food, which is the culmination of the pleasure process.

Swallowing is vitally important to tasting since after swallowing, the taste buds or receptors in the tongue continue to send information to the brain. At the same time the nasal cavity at the back of the throat receives information regarding the final smell/aroma of the food being swallowed. This is referred to as the ***finish***. But the sensation doesn't end here. How many times have you said, "What a great steak! I can still taste it and it's been over half an hour." Great food, like great wine, lasts on the palate.

Atmosphere is also essential to our sensory evaluations. Atmosphere, like smell, influences our expectations. The right atmosphere is conducive to relaxing. Relaxation opens the mind and senses. When we reach this stage, we can truly enjoy what we are experiencing. I remember tasting an excellent wine at one of my favourite vacation spots, only to be disappointed by the same wine when I tried it at home. It just didn't seem as good! The wine probably was, but the context was different.

Thus, when you go through the steps in tasting wine, keep in mind that sight, smell, taste, swallowing, finish, and atmosphere will influence your evaluation.

I offer you the following quick guide (suggestions) on how to get the most out of your wine tasting experience.

Steps in Tasting Wine

Pour a small amount of wine into a tulip shaped tasting glass. Usually a bit less than one-third full is more than enough.

Sight: Look at the liquid in the glass, preferably held up at a light or with a white background to allow the clarity and colour to be seen. Are there any floating particles? Is the wine cloudy? Is it clear? How much? Is it what you'd call brilliant like a diamond? If the wine is white, is it almost like water in colour or is there a yellowish or lemony hue to it? Or is it amber?
If it's a red wine, is it dark—almost purple and hard to see through or is it garnet in colour and quite brilliant in clarity. Is it brick red or even brown?

The colour of wine changes as it ages. An amber white colour for white wine or a brown red colour for red wine indicates oxidization due to aging. Conversely, a yellowish white or a dark purple red indicates a young wine. Certain grapes do produce different colours. For example, Pinot Noir is usually quite clear and light in colour, while Cabernet Sauvignon is dark red and almost difficult to see through when young.

Smell: Swirling the wine around in a glass exposes it to the air causing quicker oxidation, which releases the aroma[29] and bouquet.[30] After swirling, sniff lightly to obtain the aroma/bouquet but try not to overload your senses. Pause for a short moment and then sniff again to see if you sense anything else.

What do you smell? Is there a vanilla fragrance? If it's a red wine, do you note cherry or raspberry? For a white wine, do you smell cut grass, gooseberries—maybe grapefruit or lime? Is the smell pleasing? Does it encourage you to taste? These fragrances all denote desirable qualities in a wine. Older reputable wines that have been cellared properly[31] such as Bordeaux or a Canadian equivalent (Meritage, Cabernet/Merlot blend) are delicately perfumed (violets, raspberry) and elegant, while a younger or mature wine may exude powerful fruit smells such as cherry, plum, and blackberry. On the other hand, a very young wine may be considered 'closed' or exuding very little smell. What one doesn't want to smell is a 'rotten', urine, egg, sulphur and ether smell or odour. In wines that are not Sherry or Madeira, a Sherry or Madeira smell is a sure sign that the wine is oxidizing and has 'turned'.

Taste: Now take a sip. Breath in some air through your mouth and swish the wine around to obtain a sense of harmony (or not) in the wine. Does it seem overly acidic? Bitter? Is it too sweet with not enough acidity? Does the wine seem full-bodied or is it watery? Does the sugar and acidity seem balanced? Does the wine plead for you to swallow?

Swallow: Swallow the wine and exhale gently downward through your nose. This will force the bouquet through the nasal passages at the back of the throat. At the same time, a lingering sensation remains on the tongue. Count the seconds it takes for the sensation to disappear. Usually, the longer and more pleasant the sensation, the better the wine. The term used to describe this process is called the ***finish***.

Finally, consider the ***atmosphere*** in which you are tasting wine. It is conducive to opening your mind and senses to experiencing? If not, find a relaxing place where you can block out all other distractions and concentrate on what your senses are telling you.

Tasting the Food and the Wine

Surely people know how to taste wine and eat food—especially at the same time. However, amazingly, many do not get the full benefit of the tasting process. A typical meal with wine features the wine being brought to the table (and poured) prior to the food being served. By the time the food arrives, the guest(s) may have already 'tasted' several glasses and would not be able to completely enjoy the organoleptic qualities of both wine and repast together.

In addition, many people now 'enjoy' what is called 'fragmented eating'. That is, people are increasingly dinning in front of the television instead with the family at the dinning table. The television meal does not often allow for social interaction and other qualities associated with an atmosphere suitable to enjoying the full pleasure of wine and food. On the other had, eating in front of the TV is relaxing for some people.

For those occasions when you want to create a social atmosphere, here are some helpful tips.

1. If possible, have an adequately large dining table suitable for at least one more person than the guest list calls for.

2. Decide on whether the meal will feature one wine with each course or whether there will be one wine with the entire meal. If you choose the latter, you will need to consider (a) the theme and related wines and (b) alternative driving arrangements for your guests. The courses should start out with light wines and work up in weight to the main course wine and then dessert.

3. The wines should be poured with each course. First savour and taste the wine. Then taste the food along with a glass of the wine. Savour! Note the taste(s)! Then enjoy the rest of the meal at a leisurely pace.

4. The dessert wine should be as sweet or sweeter than the dessert served. The same process as the meal should be observed.

5. Conversation is the key to any culinary enjoyment. Don't make the whole evening a robotic tasting of food and wine or anything for that matter. The whole purpose of this exercise is to draw attention to what some miss when supposedly enjoying a fine meal. So take the time to Enjoy!

Selecting a Wine for that Special Dinner

I am often asked which wine should be selected for a certain meal. The answer usually is try brand X with food Y. In reality, the answer is sometimes disappointing. The disappointment comes in several ways but usually it's because the recommended wine was not liked!

1. If you are dinning by yourself, buy the wine that you like regardless of the specific food served. If you are sharing the experience with someone with a particular preference, then buy the wine they like, again, regardless of the food. Usually, the meal is finished long before the wine. Use this time to enjoy the wine on its own merits.

2. If you are planning a thematic meal, make sure to select a wine that is appropriate for the theme. For example, Maritime Cuisine would warrant a close look at the wines and foods of the Maritime Provinces. You could have several dishes from the Maritimes with accompanying wines or you could have one dish from the province with a representative wine. The same would go for the other provinces and territories in Canada. (Some more ideas for themes are provided after the following tips.)

3. The theme doesn't have to be a place, it could be a variety of grape, for example, Pinot Noir from different countries can vary in flavour, alcohol level and concentration.[32] Pinot Noir from California is very different from Burgundy, Australia, New Zealand and, of course, Canada. To accompany the Pinot Noir, select a dish from its country of origin. Again, follow the rule of lighter to heavier. The heaviest wine should be planned with the main course. The wine and food should be of equal weight and power, for instance, light Pinot goes with salmon steak and heavier Pinot works with duck.

4. Food and wine themes are great fun for dinner parties. Keep in mind that the whole purpose is to enjoy food with the wine. Too much seriousness may affect the atmosphere of the whole evening.

5. A word about sauces. Make sure to match the power of the wine with the sauce being used. A heavy sauce on a light meat such as chicken or veal can overpower the taste of the meat. Again, if the theme is a specific country or area known for its 'hot' sauces, stick to that country's wines or switch to another beverage more conducive to the food (such as Beer).

Some Additional Tips Concerning Wine/Food Pairings

1. Take into account the style of cheese when pairing it with wine. Brie or any high fat cheese needs an acidic wine such as a Riesling to 'cut the fat'. Harder goat cheese needs a tannic wine such as a Cabernet or Cabernet Blend, Shiraz or similar wine.

2. Match the strength of the wine to that of the food. As mentioned, this includes sauces—especially sauces, which can greatly alter the strength of a dish. Protein needs power usually in the form of a red wine (with the exception of eggs).

3. Similarly, when faced with a salty dish opt for a fruity wine high in acid.

4. Meat with red wine is generally over emphasized. Beef, steak, lamb and game crave powerful tasting wine, for instance, Cab Sauv, Merlot, Shiraz and Carmenere. Veal and similar meat desire lighter, gentler wines such as Pinot Noir, Gamay Noir, Sauvignon Blanc and Chardonnay (depending on sauce).

5. Chicken, especially roast chicken, is ideal for a fine red wine, but if it is topped with a cream sauce, it begs for Chardonnay, preferably barrel-aged.

6. Keep in mind that everyone is different and any organoleptic experience is bound to vary from one person to another. There are people who can identify specific wines and those who have more of a general palate. Work on your own personal experiences, descriptions and traits and use our advice simply as a guide to

assist you to develop your own preferences.

Again, there are no major rules, only suggestions. If you like it, do it!

Tips on Tasting Wine on its Own

When tasting wines of various ages start with white before red, dry before sweet and young before old. Tasting a young wine full of vibrancy (especially reds with their tannin) after trying a smooth, somewhat elegant delivery of an older wine (where the tannins have evolved into a much gentler persuasion) can destroy the earlier impression of the older red.

Dinner and Wine Tasting Themes

Dinner and/or wine tasting themes are only limited by one's imagination. Here are a few of my favourite themes.

Company Theme

Some companies have a large number of wineries under their banner. A theme concentrating a company's wine provides a convenient theme, for example, 'A Taste of Vincor' with a representative wine from each of its wineries.

Canadian Theme

A Canadian wine tasting can include a wine (or several wines) from each of the provinces along with their provincial culinary counterparts.

Provincial Theme

A specific province could also be used by having wines that represent each of the designated regions and viticultural areas of the province.

Designated Region Theme

The wines from Designated Regions within wine growing provinces can be paired along with foods from that region and province. For example,

1. Nova Scotia: (Annapolis Valley, Malagash Peninsula, Gaspereau Valley);
2. Ontario: Niagara Peninsula, Lake Erie North Shore, Pelee Island (Prince Edward County and Durham Region[33]); and
3. Quebec (Eastern Townships) British Colombia (Vancouver Island, Similkameen Valley, Okanagan Valley).

Appellation within a Region Theme

A number of Designated Regions have unique microclimates such as the Niagara Peninsula,[34] thus a possible theme could be wine(s) of the Beamsville Bench Area of the Niagara Peninsula.

Winery or Estate Theme

Self-explanatory; this theme uses the wine(s) of a particular estate or winery such as wine from Burrowing Owl Vineyards or you can select one from the list in the back of this guide book.

Designated Vineyard Theme

Finally, you could organize a dinner party around a Designated Vineyard within a winery, for instance, Chateau des Charmes: Paul Bosc Vineyard.

Thematic wine tastings and wine tasting dinners add a great deal to both the education and enjoyment of a group. The important thing is to not to get too bogged down with semantics. Most of us are not blind taste testers. We are not judges handing out medals at wine competitions. To us ordinary folk, the moment is what counts. If we can get a bit more out of our experiences, Great!

RECIPES AND WINE MATCHES

Tom Berki passionately creates unique gourmet food to suit all tastes. He has been kind enough to submit some of those recipes.

Tom Berki's Rendezvous Recipes[35]

Appetizers

A Very Garlic Bruschetta

Ingredients:

flavourful crusty bread (Foccaccia or Italian Calibrese)
2 cloves of garlic
2 tablespoons extra virgin olive oil
oregano to taste
parmesan cheese to taste
1 tomato

Process:

1. Slice the bread to desired thickness.
2. Rub the bread with a fresh clove of garlic, the more the better.
3. Brush the same bread with olive oil.
4. Sprinkle oregano and parmesan cheese.
5. Slice the tomato thinly.
6. Place one or two tomato slices on each piece of bread.
7. Sprinkle more oregano and parmesan to taste.
8. Serve.

Wine Suggestion:

For this appetizer, I suggest a wine that has the power and tannin to stand up to the garlic and tomatoes and complements the cheese and olive oil. Try *Stoney Ridge Barrel Select Baco Noir* or *Niagara College Red V.Q.A.*[36]

Creamy Cheese Stuffed Portobello Mushrooms

Ingredients:

4 large portobello mushrooms (about 6 inches in diameter)
1 cup chopped leeks (or one red onion diced)
2 tablespoons chopped parsley
¼ cup Alfredo sauce (use heavy cream as an alternative)
½ block cream cheese
¼ cup shredded Asiago cheese (or Monterey Jack if preference is milder)
3 tablespoons olive oil

Process:

1. Trim mushroom caps to 4 inches in diameter (you can use a small saucer to cut mushrooms to size).
2. Chop the stems and cut portions and reserve for filling.
3. Sauté mushroom cuttings with leeks/onions in 2 tablespoons of olive oil until tender.
4. Place in a bowl and let cool.
5. Coat the mushroom caps with a little olive oil and bake upside down or in a covered sauce pan turning every few minutes until tender.
6. Mix Alfredo sauce, cheese, parsley, sautéed mushroom cuttings and leek/onion and mix well.
7. Turn mushroom caps right side up and divide the filling (see step 6) in each of the four caps
8. Place on cookie sheet and broil until well heated.

Wine Suggestion:

A light noble wine is needed to enhance the earth flavours of mushrooms and to meld with the sauces. I recommend *Creekside Estates Cabernet.*

Easy Spinach and Crab Dip

Ingredients:

1 cup Alfred sauce
½ block of cream cheese
¼ cup Monterey cheese
1/8 cup Asiago cheese
1 can crabmeat, drained
¼ cup frozen chopped parsley, drained
2 or more pitas (toasted)

Process:

1. Mix ingredients in a bowl.
2. Heat either in microwave or in saucepan.
3. Serve with toasted pita or tacos, chips etc.

Wine Suggestion:

When in doubt as to the wine, select a fine sparkling wine with fine flavours and bubbles and enough acidity to cut through the cream *or* choose the great flavours of fruit wines. I suggest trying *Chateau des Charmes 'Sec' Sparkling Wine*[37] or *Fieldstone Fruit Wines 'Bumbleberry Fruit Wine'*.[38]

Tom Berki's Rendezvous Recipes[35]

Main Courses

Smoked Salmon Asparagus Wraps with Creamy Dill Aioli

Ingredients (serves two):

12 fresh asparagus spears, blanched and cooled
4 slices smoked salmon
½ cup Alfredo sauce
4 tablespoons finely chopped dill
2 teaspoons tarragon

Process:

1. Wrap six asparagus spears in two slices of smoked salmon.
2. Repeat step one with the remaining asparagus and salmon.
3. Combine the other ingredients.
4. Warm ingredients in either microwave or saucepan.
5. Pour over the bundles.

Wine Suggestion:

The fruity acidity of a Riesling or the crisp fruitiness of a Rose is a fine match for the above. My choice of wine for this dish is Angels Gate Riesling *or* Wine Garden Estate Rose.

Salmon and Seafood with Citrus Wine Sauce

If you're a fish or seafood lover, it's the citrus wine sauce, which adds a new dimension to this dish.

Ingredients (serves 4):

6oz boneless salmon fillets
fresh shrimp
fresh scallops
2 cups citrus wine sauce (see sauce recipe)
salt and pepper to taste

Process:

1. Coat salmon with a little butter, season with salt and pepper.
2. Grill, fry, or bake your salmon.
3. Cook at medium heat until it is medium/well (the salmon will be juicy).
4. Sautee shrimp and scallops in a frying pan with a little butter (about 1 tablespoon).
5. Add a little salt and pepper. Cook on medium heat until the shrimp barely turns pink and the scallops turn an opaque colour.
6. Add citrus wine sauce and warm through.
7. Place cooked salmon on a plate and ladle sauce.
8. Divide shrimp and scallops equally.
9. Add your favourite starch and vegetables.

Suggested Wine:

An elegant white wine with a good background of fruit and tropical flavours pairs well with the citrus, butter and tropical flavours of mango and pineapple. If you prefer red wine, pick one that is not too heavy but is fruity and has a touch of herbal elegance. With this dish you will enjoy *Jackson-Triggs Grande Reserve Chardonnay or Kacaba Vineyards Pinot Noir.*

Pecan Crusted Rack of Lamb

This is a very easy, elegant dish that is sure to amaze your friends.

Ingredients:

2 racks of lamb, each with ten ribs, 'Frenched'[39]
2 cups of pecans
½ teaspoon of ground cumin
¼ cup red wine
¼ cup beef stock

Process:

1. Season lamb with salt and pepper.
2. Rub the lamb with Dijon mustard (this is the secret!).
3. Make sure to coat all meat surfaces with this mustard.
4. In a food processor grind about 2 cups of pecans to the consistency of coarse breadcrumbs.
5. Place the ground pecans in a dry frying pan and toast over medium heat stirring or shaking the pan constantly until you smell the aromas from the pecans (this will release their essential oils and enhance their flavour).
6. Let the pecans cool to room temperature. Add the ground cumin, stir and coat the meat with the pecan mixture.
7. In a large fry pan heat enough oil to barely cover the pan.
8. Add lamb racks and brown one side.
9. Turn over and brown the other side.
10. Finish the racks in the oven.
11. We suggest cooking until it is medium to medium-rare for 10 to 12 minutes at 400°F, depending on the size of your racks.
12. Use a meat thermometer to verify your optimum cooking temperature.
13. Remove from oven, tent with foil and let rest for 5 to 10 minutes.

For the sauce, use the same pan you cooked with. This recipe serves 4 people.

1. Drain the fat.
2. Add the following:
   ¼ cup of dry red wine to the frying pan,
   ¼ cup of beef stock,
   1 tablespoon of mint jelly.
3. Bring to a boil and simmer for 5 minutes.
4. Ladle over the lamb.
5. Cut Chops between each rib.
6. Serve with garlic mashed potatoes and steamed vegetables.

Suggested Wine:

If I were a rack of lamb, let me marry a wine of spice and power that can handle the fat and complement the mint while providing mouthfuls of refined pleasure. With this dish, I enjoy *Konzelmann Cabernet/Merlot* and *Osoyoos-Larose.*

Roasted Red Pepper Cream Chicken

I always wonder what to do with the bland taste of chicken. Tom says, "This recipe will make *you* a gourmet cook!"

Ingredients (serves 2):

2 boneless, skinless chicken breasts (each about 4 to 5 oz)
½ cup sauce (Alfredo sauce—see sauces)
2 tablespoons grated Asiago cheese
¼ cup roasted red peppers coarsely chopped

Process:

1. Cook the chicken breasts thoroughly.
2. Add the cheese to the roasted peppers.
2. Heat thoroughly in a sauté pan.
3. Before plating, add 2 tablespoons of either chopped fresh baby spinach or thawed, drained chopped spinach.
4. Spoon over each chicken breast and serve with rice or noodles.

Suggested Wine:

What wine goes with pepper and spice? The sauce, which is cream, goes with wine that's a dream. Try *Nk'Mip Cellars Qwam Qwant Merlot* or *Orofino Vineyard Merlot.*

Crispy coatings

If it's juicy food that you like, try these tips.

1. *Half and Half.* Instead of breadcrumbs, try adding half breadcrumbs and half pecans on chicken or pork for a different flavor.

2. *Dijon Mustard.* Try coating lamb chops with Dijon mustard and season with cracked black pepper and chopped pecans.

3. *Almonds,* whether chopped or shaved be sure to toast them slightly in a dry frying pan first to release their essential oils. Then dip either whole or filleted trout in a mixture of beaten eggs making sure that the fish is well coated with the almonds. Bake or fry until the fish is done.

4. *Croutons.* For something truly unique, use ½ seasoned croutons and ½ bread crumbs for a different flavor. Simply place your croutons in a plastic bag and shake lightly.

Tips of the day

If you're breading veal or chicken for a Parmesan dish, add a couple tablespoons of Parmesan and oregano to your breading mixture.

When breading any meat, season the breading with a little onion powder, garlic powder, thyme and chopped parsley. If you're watching your salt intake this will create a new taste to help reduce your sodium while adding tremendous flavour to your breading.

Tom Berki's Rendezvous Recipes[35]

Soups

Homemade Potato and Leek Soup

Ingredients:

2 lbs of pealed quartered potato or use a high starch variety such as Russet or baking potato.
2 leeks, chopped white part, leave the green part whole.
½ cup chopped onion
2 bay leafs
2 cloves garlic
¼ teaspoon thyme
2 cups chicken stock or broth
2 cups 35% cream
4 tablespoons butter
2 tablespoons corn starch
1 tablespoons salt

Process:

1. In a heavy pot over medium heat, sauté chopped onion, garlic and white part of leeks (washed and chopped) in butter until tender.
3. Add potato (washed and pealed), whole green part of leeks and chicken broth.
4. Add water to bring the liquid level to 1 inch above the potatoes.
5. Add salt and bay leaves, cover and bring to a boil.
6. Then reduce to simmer and cook until the potatoes are very tender.
7. Remove and discard the green part of leeks and bay leaves.
8. With a hand blender, blend soup until smooth or use a potato masher if you prefer it with a little texture.
9. Add cream and bring back to heat.
10. Add cornstarch with ¼ cup of water and simmer until thickened. For a thicker soup add more cornstarch mixture.
11. For a vegetarian version, omit chicken stock: use water of vegetable stock. Check the seasoning to taste.
12. Serve with garlic-toasted bread.

Suggested Wine:

A bit of sweet can be neat. Try the slightly sweet and acidic Riesling or a great fruit wine such as *Ocala Orchards Riesling* or *La Ferme Bourgeois 'Beausejour'*.

Cream of Mushroom Soup

Ingredients:

2 lbs of button mushrooms
1 large portobello mushroom
¼ cup chopped onion
4 tablespoons butter
1 oz sherry
1 cup chicken broth or stock
2 cups of 35% cream
2 tablespoons corn starch
1 teaspoon salt

Process:

1. In a heavy pot, sauté onion until tender.
2. Reserve 1 cup of sliced button mushrooms. Coarsely chop the remaining mushrooms including the stems and add to the pot.
3. Add chicken broth or stock.
4. Add water to just cover the mushroom.
5. Bring soup to a boil, reduce to a simmer and cook for 45 minutes.
6. With a hand blender, purée soup until smooth, add sherry and cream.
7. Mix cornstarch with ¼ cup of water and add to soup. Bring the soup to a high simmer while stirring until it slightly thickens.
8. In a frying pan, sauté sliced mushrooms with 1 tablespoon of butter until almost tender, add to soup and stir.
9. For a thicker soup repeat cornstarch mixture.
10. Taste and adjust seasoning.

Suggested Wine:

With this soup I like *Hawthorne Mountain Pinot Gris* or *Peninsula Ridge Chardonnay Reserve.*

Cream of Butternut Squash

Ingredients:

2 lbs of butternut squash, pealed and seeded
1 cup of chicken broth or stock
2 cups 35% cream
½ teaspoon nutmeg
1 teaspoon salt
1 tablespoon cornstarch

Process:

1. Cut squash into chunks and place in a large pot.
2. Add chicken broth.
3. Add enough water to cover squash by 1 inch.
4. Add nutmeg.
5. Bring soup to a boil then reduce to simmer and cook until squash is tender.
6. Purée with a hand blender until very smooth.
7. Mix corn starch with ¼ cup of water add to soup.
8. Add cream and reheat.
9. Taste and adjust seasoning.

Suggested Wine:

A wine that meets the challenge of the squash while matching the power of the cream will surely make the meal something of a dream! *Sumac Ridge Cellar Select Sauvignon Blanc* or *Blasted Church Hatfield's Fuse White*[40] will suit your dinner fine.

Tom Berki's Rendezvous Recipes[35]

Easy Sauces[41]

Mmm! Sauces so good, and so easy to make!

Alfredo Sauce

Ingredients:

1 litre of 18% cream
½ litre cold milk
¼ cup melted butter
1 tablespoon powdered chicken base
1 teaspoon garlic powder
1 teaspoon onion powder
4 tablespoons parmesan cheese
3 tablespoons cornstarch
1 cup cold milk
favourite pasta

Process:

1. Heat butter, cream and milk to scalding point.
2. Combine with garlic powder, onion powder, and parmesan cheese.
3. Finish by mixing 1 cup cold milk with 3 tablespoons of cornstarch.
4. Add to hot cream mixture. Stir while heating until thick (you can thicken the sauce further by either cooking the sauce until it reduces or by adding more corn starch to the mixture).
5. Serve with your favourite pasta, or create a Rose' sauce by adding equal amounts of marinara sauce (see below).

Suggested Wine Type:

> *Fruit, spice and crisp acidity from any wine will surely keep Alfredo from getting saucy.*

I recommend Barrel Aged Chardonnay, Riesling or Gewurztraminer.

Marinara Sauce

Ingredients:

3lbs tomatoes (preferably canned)[42]
1 cup chopped onions
4 cloves of garlic—more if you like garlic
2 bay leaves
1 tablespoon of oregano
1 tablespoon dried basil
2 tablespoons tomato paste
¼ cup of red wine such as a Merlot[43]
6 tablespoons of olive oil (virgin to extra virgin)
salt and pepper to taste

Process:

1. The secret to a great sauce is to partially purée or chop your tomatoes.
2. In a heavy pot over medium temperature, heat the olive oil and sauté the onions and garlic until tender.
4. Add remaining ingredients, cover and bring to a boil.
5. Reduce to a simmer, stirring occasionally for 1 hour.
6. Serve with your favourite pasta.

Suggested Wine Type:

Tomatoes, garlic and onions call for a red wine. Try this sauce with *Merlot, Cabernet or Gamay.*

Roasted Red Pepper Sauce

If you're tired of tomato sauce, here's a new spin on red sauce.

Ingredients:

4 cups of roasted red peppers (use canned variety not pickled in vinegar)
4 cloves fresh garlic
1 bay leaf
salt and pepper to taste
½ cup chopped onion
¼ cup red wine (preferably Merlot)
1 tablespoon tomato paste
1 tablespoon oregano

Process:

1. Purée the red peppers until the peppers are the size of corn kernels.
2. Sauté the onion and garlic in oil until tender.
3. Add the remainder of the ingredients.
4. Bring it to a boil and reduce to a simmer for 20 minutes.
5. Add this to pasta or over top chicken or fish.

> **Tip of the day.** Here's another twist. Try using equal amounts of Alfredo sauce and roasted red pepper cream sauce over chicken or pasta. Experiment with your own blend to taste.

Suggested Wine Type:

Power hath its needs. This sauce demands it without question.

I like either *Merlot, Cabernet or Shiraz.*[44]

Citrus Fruit Sauce

This sauce is recommended over chicken or fish.

Ingredients:

¼ cup each of chopped red, green and yellow bell pepper
¼ cup chopped red onion
1 clove garlic chopped
¼ cup butter
¼ cup grapefruit juice
¼ cup apple juice
1½ cups orange juice
2 tablespoons flour
2 tablespoons lemon juice
2 tablespoons lime juice
1 tablespoon brown sugar
2 tablespoons chopped parsley
¼ cup white wine, preferably a Sauvignon Blanc[45]
½ cup of your favourite dried fruit (cherries, apples, raisins, etc)

Process:

1. Sauté pepper, onions and garlic in butter until tender.
2. Add flour and stir for 5 minutes.
3. Add other ingredients and bring to a boil for 10 minutes.

Tip of the day. To vary the taste of citrus fruit sauce, try the following.

Citrus and Wine Sauce

Ingredients:

1 cup chopped bell peppers (use different colourations for effect)
¼ cup chopped red onions
2 cloves garlic
1 cup orange juice
1 tablespoon capers (optional)
¼ cup white wine (preferably unoaked)
1 tablespoon chopped parsley
½ cup grapefruit juice
½ cup apple juice
juice from ½ a lemon
½ cup of a lime juice
1 teaspoon brown sugar
1 tablespoon cornstarch
2 tablespoons butter
4 tablespoons water

Process:

1. Sauté onions, garlic and bell peppers until translucent.
2. Add all other ingredients and boil.
3. Let simmer for 15 minutes.
4. Add cornstarch and water then bring to boil (this thickens the sauce).
5. Serve over grilled chicken, fish and even veal.

Suggested Wine Type:

> *Herbal and crisp dryness hath their uses. A wine with both seldom looses.*

I prefer *Sauvignon Blanc, Unoaked Chardonnay* or *Viognier*

Stir Fry Sauce

This is a versatile sauce. It goes well with stir-fries, and you can use it to marinade chicken, beef or pork.

Ingredients:

1 cup plum sauce
1 cup sweet chili sauce
4 tablespoons soya sauce
pinch of thyme
1 bay leaf
1 clove of chopped garlic
1/8 cup of white wine, oaked Chardonnay[46]

Process:

1. Add all ingredients to a saucepot and simmer for 15 minutes.
2. Use as a topping for stir-fries, fowl, white and red meats.

> **Tip of the day**. If serving red meats, one option is to replace the Chardonnay with a big bold red such as Cabernet Sauvignon or Cab/Merlot blend.

Suggested Wine Type:

Colour of wine need not worry. It's the meal that chooses the company! Use the wines mentioned in the recipe.

Jerk Sauce

You can make this versatile zesty sauce as hot or mild as you like.

Ingredients:

½ cup chopped onion
4 cloves chopped garlic
¼ cup each of chopped green, yellow and red pepper
1 medium tomato peeled, seeded and chopped
¼ teaspoon cayenne pepper
1 bay leaf
½ teaspoon of thyme
1 to 4 teaspoons of any brand of jerk seasoning
(The above amount depends of your level of heat)
2 cups beef stock
2 tablespoons flour
2 tablespoons olive oil (for sautéing)

Process:

1. Sauté onion and garlic and peppers in oil until tender.
2. Add flour, stir and cook for 5 minutes.
3. Add tomatoes and cook until they break down.
4. Add remaining ingredients, bring to a boil and simmer for 20 minutes.
5. Reduce to desired consistency.

Suggested Wine Type:

> *Peppers three and spice without question, somewhat challenging,*
> *but a spicy white wine or beer may be the bastion.*

Depending on how much of the sauce is used, try a spicy wine such as Gewürztraminer. Or for an alternative, there's nothing like a cold lager ale or beer with spicy food.[47]

Compote

Compote is a multi-purpose sauce ideal for veal or pork or breaded fried cheese.

Ingredients:

1 cup of frozen or fresh blueberries
1 cup of raspberries or cranberries
1 cup of water
2 tablespoons sugar (amount optional)
1 oz Frangellico

Process:

1. Add sugar, 2 tablespoons at a time until desired sweetness is obtained.
2. Cook on medium heat to reduced slightly until thick and syrupy.
3. Serve with above dishes.

Suggested Wine Type:

> *Fruit begets fruit and sweetness so rare. With a hint of acidity, a flowery wine can tame any bear! Depending on sweetness (and the entrée), select a medium dry to sweet Riesling or fruit wine.*

Creamy Cheesy Dip

Cheese dips are always a party favourite. Use this creamy dip with vegetables, shrimp, crab, or smoked salmon.

Ingredients:

1 cup of Alfredo sauce (see recipe)
1 cup cream cheese
1 tablespoon parsley
1/8 cup chopped spinach

Process:

1. Mix all ingredients together and microwave until warm.
2. Serve with toasted pita bread or crackers.

Suggested Wine Type:

> *Cheese and cream! Add fish too! A fruity red wine, maybe a white, depending on taste, a marguerita may do!*

Gamay Noir, Pinot Gris or Cocktails

Navan Chicken

'Navan' is a new cognac liqueur produced by Grand Marnier. Instead of adding oranges to cognac they blend the finest vanilla beans from Madagascar with their own cognac for a truly unique taste.

Ingredients:

8 boneless and skinless chicken breasts fully cooked
3 cups of our Alfredo sauce (see recipe)
3 tablespoons butter
3 oz of Navan Liqueur
1/8 cup chopped red onion
1 fresh banana sliced
rice pilaf
your favourite vegetables
salt and pepper to taste

Process:

1. Sauté red onion in the butter over medium heat until tender.
2. Add Alfredo sauce.
3. REMOVE[48] pan from heat and add Navan.
4. Stir and place pan back on heat.
5. Warm to a simmer for 5 minutes to burn away alcohol.
6. Add sliced banana.
7. Spoon the sauce over chicken breast. Serve with rice pilaf and your favourite vegetables.

Suggested Wine:

> *Truly a noble dish made for a royal drink like that of Sir Navan. If not he, then strength of sweetness and smell of grapefruit rare or the trusty sweet and somewhat acidic tongue with German flare!*

Try sipping *Navan* in a liqueur glass or have a *Cave Spring Cellars Medium Dry Riesling* or *Jost Vineyards Muscat Icewine.*

Chicken Picata with Citrus and Wine Sauce

Ingredients:

4-5 oz fresh, skinless, boneless chicken breasts
4 large eggs
1 teaspoon fresh chopped parsley
1 teaspoon thyme
1 teaspoon oregano
1 teaspoon garlic powder
2 tablespoons parmesan cheese
1 ½ cups citrus and wine sauce
4 tablespoons chopped tomato
4 tablespoons chopped spinach
4 tablespoons chopped green onion
salt and pepper to taste
olive oil[49]

Process:

1. Beat eggs with mixer adding the parmesan and herbs.
2. Season chicken with salt and pepper and dip into mixture.
3. Place into sauté pan with oil.
4. Sizzle chicken for one minute then turn over.
5. Place in preheated oven at 350° F to finish cooking (until brown)—juices should run clear (no pink should remain).

Tip of the day. Buy 1 or 2 bunches of fresh parsley. The flat leaf variety is best. Wash parsley very well in cold water. Shake off excess water. Tear in half and place into a food processor. Pulse processor until the parsley is chopped. Then, place in an airtight container and put in the freezer. When you need parsley, go to the freezer, open the container and scrape the parsley with a fork to add to your dish, refreeze unused portion for next time.

Sauce

1. Bring citrus and wine sauces to a boil
2. Add chopped tomato, spinach and green onion
3. Taste for tenderness
4. Ladle over chicken when ready

Suggested Wine:

Chicken and citrus with two great wines—each white yet different but both with herbal zest, melding with the chicken and all the rest!

Mission Hill Pinot Blanc or Malevoire Sauvignon Blanc

Tom Berki's Rendezvous Recipes

Pastas

Fettuccine Alfredo

This is a classic favourite. Try a new variation of this dish.

Ingredients:

Alfredo sauce[50]
fettuccine
parmesan cheese
ground black pepper
red onion
red and yellow bell peppers

Process:

1. Boil and prepare pasta.
2. Sauté red onion and peppers.
3. Heat and add Alfredo sauce to the above.
4. Ladle over prepared fettuccine.
5. Sprinkle with grated parmesan and pepper.

Wine Suggestion:

Creamy sauce with all its splendour! Mixed with onions, peppers, cheese and pasta—No wonder! A white so round with power and flavour is required here to overcome a salty endeavour!

Pillitteri Estates Vidal or *Henry of Pelham Barrel Fermented Chardonnay*

Caribbean Pasta

This recipe will make you feel like your vacationing at the Islands. If you like jerk and seafood, try them on pasta for a change.

Ingredients:

Pasta (any kind)
8 oz of fresh salmon filet
10 fresh scallops, more if you prefer
1 ½ cups jerk sauce recipe
1 cup Marinara[51] sauce recipe
¼ cup chopped red onion
½ green pepper chopped
½ yellow pepper chopped
1/8 cup chopped parsley
2 oz dry white wine
1 fresh jalapeno pepper chopped (if you like it hot)
olive oil

Process:

1. Sauté onions and peppers in oil until just barely tender.
2. Add salmon and scallops and wine and cook through, add parsley, jerk sauce and marinara sauce.
3. Heat thoroughly.
4. Serve over your favourite pasta.

Wine Suggestion:

> *"Eyrie man!" Says the man on the tropical beach. "Get some hot stuff that don't cause yo' tummy no stitch! For sure! 'Cause the cool pink wine o' spicy white will help to please the coming night!".*

Township 7 Vineyards and Winery Rose V.Q.A. or *Sonoran Estate Winery Gewurztraminer*

Thai Stir Fry

Ingredients:

stir fry sauce[52]
Nappa cabbage
bean sprouts
assorted peppers (green, yellow, red)
onion
snow peas
steamed cooked rice

Process:

1. Make stir fry sauce as per recipe (try using Nova Scotia's L'Acadie Blanc Wine in the Sauce or similar wine).
2. Depending on number of guests, steam cook one/two cups of rice.
3. In a separate pan, heat one tablespoon of olive oil.
4. Add vegetables chopped to taste.
5. Stir fry to personal taste—usually 5 to 8 minutes.
6. Place vegetables over rice.
7. Add stir fry sauce over top of vegetables and rice.

Wine Suggestion:

> *The wine from within chooses the wine from without, along with the food it will dictate the clout! White with white and red with red—both avail! Spice in the red must prevail.*

Jost, Gaspereau or *Grand Pre L'Acadie Blanc* or *Mission Hill S.L.C. Syrah*[53]

Tip of the day. For variety, one can add chicken and or beef to the stir-fry.

Wineries' Signature Dishes

A wise man once said, "Eat, drink, and be merry!" We should not be surprised to find that the winemakers and their staff were so gracious to donate their recipes—tried, tested and true.

Archibald Orchards Cranberry Roast

Ingredients:

4 lbs sirloin tip, inside round or eye of round roast
1 can jelly cranberry sauce
2 finely chopped onions
3 tablespoons soy sauce
3 tablespoons Archibald Orchards Cranberry Wine
1 teaspoon ground ginger

Process:

1. Heat ingredients (other than roast) in sauté pan until smooth.
2. Place roast fat side up in open pan.
3. Spread sauce mixture on roast. Reserve half of the sauce.
4. Place roast, open pan, in a preheated 275°F oven for 2 hours or until done.
6. Slice the finished roast thinly across the grain.
7. Serve meat with remaining heated sauce.

Suggested Wine:

> *A juicy roast, medium or rare, with fruit wine added makes a taste so round—enough to please a bear! With fruit sweetness and acid—with care! Well done, medium rare!*

Archibald Orchards' Apple Cranberry

D'Angelo Estates Winery Quick Potato and Pasta Dishes

These are two basic dishes that are very easy and quick to make and can complement many main courses and most wines.

Sal's Quick Potato and Garlic

Ingredients:

potatoes (two per person)
garlic (to taste)
olive oil (1-2 tablespoons)
salt and pepper (as needed)

Process:

1. Boil potatoes.
2. Finely chop the garlic.
3. Heat in olive oil.
4. Mix all the ingredients.
5. Add salt and pepper.

Suggested Wine:

A Mediterranean grape it should be,
caress the olives,
the garlic,
and potatoes you see.

D'Angelo Estates Malbec

D'Angelo Estates Quick Pasta

Ingredients:

pasta (any kind)
fresh garlic (to taste)
1-2 tablespoons of olive oil
salt and pepper (to taste)

Process:

1. Boil pasta.
2. Finely chop garlic.
3. Heat in olive oil.
4. Mix all ingredients.
5. Add salt and pepper.

Wine Suggestion:

A wine with lightness elegant can dress this meal that has pleased many and inspire a taste supreme!

D'Angelo Estate Pinot Noir

Township 7 Wild Mushroom Risotto[54]

Ingredients:

1 large white onion (diced)
1 garlic clove (minced)
2 cups Arborio Rice
1 tablespoon fresh oregano (finely chopped)
1 tablespoon fresh thyme (finely chopped)
1 cup fresh button mushrooms
1 cup oyster mushrooms
1 cup shitake mushrooms
hot chicken stock or water

Process:

1. Sauté diced onion and garlic in olive oil in a saucepan until translucent (about 6 minutes). Stir frequently.
2. Add fresh herbs and continue to stir for another minute.
3. Add the rice and four cups of stock or water.
4. Stir constantly until the rice has absorbed most of the liquid. Continue adding liquid until the rice is cooked 'al dente' (still crisp).
5. Set the rice aside off the heat. Sauté the mushrooms in olive oil in a separate pan.
6. Add the rice to the sautéed mushrooms and add four ounces of Township 7 Vineyards and Winery Chardonnay.
7. Stir a minute over low heat. The rice should have a creamy texture at this stage. If necessary, add a bit of liquid to the mixture.
8. Season to taste with salt, white pepper, parmesan cheese and butter.

This risotto is a perfect accompaniment to warm bread and shaved parmesan cheese.

Wine Suggestion:

The wine—a bit of butter, some apple with grapefruit on the side will surly take the risotto along for the ride. The flavours of the wine, with both mushroom and rice, will complement the salt, cheese and added spice. A royal feast to endure and please all for sure!

Township 7 Vineyards and Winery Chardonnay

Notre Dame[55] 'Twillingate' Baked Fillets with Crispy Cheese Topping

Ingredients:

2 lbs fresh or thawed fish fillets
½ teaspoon salt
1/8 teaspoon pepper
3 cups soft bread cubes
6 tablespoons butter/olive oil or other fat
1 cup chopped onion
1 teaspoon dry mustard
1 cup grated cheddar cheese
¼ cup parsley

Process:

1. Season fillets in salt and pepper and place in baking pan.
2. Toast bread cubes.
3. Melt butter and add onion.
4. Cover and cook until tender (about 5 minutes).
5. Stir in mustard.
6. Combine toasted bread cubes with onion mixture.
7. Add cheese and parsley.
8. Toss gently until well mixed.
9. Spread topping over fillets.
10. Bake at 350°F for 20 to 25 minutes until fish flakes easily with a fork test.

Wine Suggestion:

A meal from an isle requires a wine of local flare.
One that senses the fish an' all that's there.
Made from a berry that grows near the beaches.
Its fruit gives greetings to all it reaches.

Notre Dame Black Crowberry[56]

Bed & Breakfasts

Devonshire Inn[57] On The Lake 'Chicken Liver Pate'

Ingredients (makes 2 cups):

6 tablespoons sweet butter
½ cup finely minced yellow onion
2 garlic cloves, peeled & chopped
1 teaspoon dried thyme
½ cup celery tops
10 black peppercorns
2 bay leaves
6 cups water
1 pound chicken livers
2 tablespoons cognac
½ teaspoon salt
½ teaspoon ground allspice
5 teaspoons water-packed green peppercorns, drained
¼ cup heavy cream

Process:

1. Melt the butter in a skillet. Add the onion, garlic and thyme. Cook covered over medium heat for about 25 minutes or until onion is tender and lightly coloured.
2. In a saucepan containing 6 cups of water add the celery-tops, peppercorns and bay leaves. Bring to a boil, reduce heat and simmer for 10 minutes.
3. Add chicken livers to the saucepan (step 2) and simmer for 10 minutes. Livers should be slightly pink inside.
4. Drain livers and discard the celery-tops, bay leaves and peppercorns. Place livers with butter and garlic in the bowl of a food processor fitted with a steel blade. Add cognac, salt, pepper, allspice and 4 teaspoons of green peppercorns.
5. Pour in the cream and process again to blend. Transfer to a bowl and stir in remaining teaspoon of green peppercorns.
6. Scrape mixture into a 2-cup terrine. Cover and refrigerate for at least 4 hours before serving.
7. Let pate stand at room temperature for at least 30 minutes prior to serving.

Wine Suggestion:

> *The Black Prince hath his livers, spicy and bold. Royalty wished its legendary palate secure. With pepper and spice a youthful, zesty and fruity wine will endure.*

Grange of Prince Edward County, 'Trumpour's Mill Gamay Noir'

Grand Victorian's[58] *Baked Orange French Toast*

Ingredients:

3 tablespoons freshly grated orange zest
2 cups fresh orange juice
¼ cup sugar
¼ teaspoon vanilla
2 tablespoons 'Glayva' or Grand Marnier Liqueur
6 large eggs
½ half & half cream
8 one-inch thick diagonal slices 'Challah' or quality
Italian bread
3 tablespoons unsalted butter, melted
1 pinch of salt

Sauce:

3 tablespoons unsalted butter
2 tablespoons sweet orange marmalade
1 tablespoon 'Glayva'[59] or Grand Marnier Liqueur

Process:

1. In a large bowl, whisk together zest, juice, sugar, vanilla, Glayva, eggs, half & half cream and salt.
2. In a 9 x 13 x 2 inch glass baking dish, arrange the bread slices in a single layer.
3. Pour the mixture over the bread, turning slices over to cover and chill. Cover for 4 hours or overnight.
4. Pre-heat oven to 400°F and brush large baking sheet with butter.
5. Using a slotted spatula, arrange bread in one layer on the baking sheet, leaving room between slices and bake in the middle of the oven for 5 minutes.
6. Rotate pan and bake for 5 minutes more.
7. Turn over bread, bake for 5 more minutes and repeat rotation for another 5 minutes. Bread should be puffed and golden when done.
8. While the bread is baking, place the *sauce* material into a saucepan and cook but-

ter, marmalade and Glayva on low heat and stir until butter is melted.
9. Drizzle the French toast with sauce and serve with syrup.

Suggested Wine:

Sweetness roams around vintage with flowers, honey and peach. Adding sweet Scottish herb or orange yearns for apricot to match.

Reif Estates Vidal Select Late Harvest

Twin Oaks Baked Egg and Cheese

Ingredients:

10 eggs
1 cup milk
½ cup cream
2 teaspoons sugar
1 cup shredded Monterey Jack, Muenster or cheddar cheese
4 ounces cream, cubed or feta cheese
½ cup cottage cheese
½ cup salsa
1½ tablespoon ketchup
1½ teaspoon mustard
2/3 cup melted butter, melted margarine or olive oil
2/3 cup flour
2 teaspoons baking powder
salt, pepper, garlic, onion powder to taste
herbs such as basil and/or parsley to taste

Process:

1. Beat together eggs, milk and sugar.
2. Add cheese, melted butter or oil with sauces and mix well.
3. Mix in flour and baking powder.
4. Pour into a baking dish sprayed with non-stick pan coating.
5. Bake 45 to 50 minutes in preheated oven at 350°F. Check by inserting knife in centre. If it comes out clean, the meal is ready.
6. Meal may be prepared for cooking in advance. Just cover and store in refrigerator until required for cooking. When ready, cook uncovered for 60 minutes.
7. Keep in mind that ovens vary so check after 40 minutes. Also remember that the dish will continue to cook if left in a hot baking pan even if removed from oven.
8. Cut into rectangles and serve when ready.
9. This recipe can be varied to include chopped broccoli, diced tomatoes, different types of cheeses, and even different sauces such as barbeque sauce and black bean sauce.

Wine Suggestion:

> *Waking up is fun to do when faced with a meal with cheese and one egg or two. A fancy drink with bubbles may be for you while others desire a touch of sweet citrus too!*

Sparkling Wine mixed with Orange Juice for Breakfast or *a Pelee Island Blanc de Blanc Seyval/Vidal*

Antler Creek 'Easy Stroganoff'

Ingredients (serves 4-6 persons):

1½ lb round steak
3 tablespoons flour
½ teaspoon salt
1/8 teaspoon pepper
¼ cup vegetable oil
1½ cup beef stock or bouillon
1¼ cup chopped onion
1 can sliced mushrooms (undrained)
1 teaspoon Worcestershire sauce
3 tablespoons red wine
1 cup sour cream

Process:

1. Cut steak into strips.
2. Dredge meat in flour seasoned with salt and pepper.
3. In a large pan, brown meat in preheated oil.
4. Add stock, onions, mushrooms and Worcestershire sauce.
5. Simmer for 30 minutes on low heat until meat is tender and sauce has thickened.
6. Remove from heat.
7. Blend in wine and sour cream.
8. Heat thoroughly, but do not boil.
9. Serve over rice or with rice.[60]

Wine Suggestion:

> *The same wine in cooking is used for drinking is the adage! A red wine young and alive will help you manage!*

Naked Grape Shiraz[61]

Chefs/Restaurants

Chef Roberto Fracchioni[62]
Millcroft Inn
Three Course Menu

First Course: Heirloom Tomato Salad

Ingredients:

½ Vidella onion
½ tablespoon butter
1 heirloom tomato
¼ tablespoon roasted garlic
¼ tablespoon fresh garlic, very finely chopped
1 tablespoon fresh basil, washed and finely chopped
1 tablespoon fresh parsley, washed, picked and chopped
1 tablespoon good olive oil
¼ tablespoon balsamic vinegar
salt and pepper to taste

Process:

1. Cut Vidella onion into one-eighth inch square dice.
2. Place in heavy bottom pan with butter over low heat.
3. Slowly cook onions until brown and caramelized.
4. Set aside and cool.
5. Cut heirloom tomato into one-eighth inch square pieces.
6. Mix tomatoes with all ingredients and season to taste.

Suggested Wine:

> *Fresh tomatoes, onions and vinegar abound making a need for assertion. These wines below can move well among them without any recession.*

Longdog Pinot Grigio or *Southbrook Winery White*

Second Course: Prince Edward Island Mussels

(With pearl onion, double smoked bacon, tomato and steamed Eisbock)

Ingredients:

2 tablespoons olive oil
2 cloves minced garlic
2 cups Eisbock Beer or any dark beer
1¾ cups pearl onions, cleaned
1½ cups diced, double smoked bacon
2 ½ cups diced tomatoes
2 sprigs of thyme, picked and chopped
2 sprigs of marjoram picked and chopped
6 lbs of mussels, cleaned and de-bearded

Process:

1. Place oil in pot and add bacon.
2. Cook over low heat to render the fat.
3. Turn heat to high and when hot add mussels, garlic, onions, tomatoes and herbs.
4. Sauté ingredients for two or three minutes.
5. Add beer, cover pot and cook for 6 or 7 minutes.
6. Serve when mussels are open.

Wine Suggestion:

> *A meal so special must be served with special wines—*
> *one with butter, vanilla, the other with melon, mango and banana.*
> *A beer may also delight. All three will bring great joy whether had*
> *by girl or boy!*

Rossignol Estate Winery Ortega Chardonnay[63] or
Inniskillin Montague Estate Pinot Gris

Third Course: Seared Sterling Silver Flat Iron Steak in Bourbon-Prune Butter Sauce

Ingredients:

6 pieces Sterling Silver Flatiron Steak (each about 7 oz)
4 tablespoons unsalted butter
1 tablespoon olive oil
1 tablespoon fresh thyme washed, picked and chopped
1 tablespoon fresh sage washed, picked and chopped
3 oz bourbon
1 piece shallot, diced
6 pieces dried prunes, finely diced
salt and pepper to taste

Process:

1. Marinate the steaks overnight in oil, thyme and sage.
2. Heat a heavy bottom pan (preferably cast iron) until hot.
3. Sprinkle the meat with some salt and pepper.
4. Add half of the butter to pan (it should melt and turn brown quickly).
5. Add the steaks to the pan and cook over high heat until you see juices rising to the top (usually about 5-7 minutes).
6. Turn steaks over and cook another 5 minutes.
7. Remove steaks and set aside in warm place.
8. Turn stove down to low and remove pan from heat.
9. Let the pan cool for 2-3 minutes then add the bourbon, prunes and shallots (Be careful the alcohol may ignite. Let it burn itself out—3 to 6 seconds).
10. Let the liquid in the pan cook until it is almost all gone (about 2 minutes).
11. Remove the pan from the stove and slowly whisk in remaining butter.
12. Serve steaks and cover them with sauce from pan.

Wine Suggestion:

> *T'is a serious choice with meat so tender. It cries out in voice for a wine with the colour of red with pepper, berries, and plums in good stead.*

Burrowing Owl Cabernet Sauvignon[64] or
Crown Bench Estates Merlot

Chef Alex Jurt[65]
Le Caveau Restaurant
Grand Pre Vineyards

Scallop with Curry and Banana

Ingredients: (Basic)

36 scallops
1 banana
600 ml curry sauce (about 2 ½ cups)
Basmati rice
curry sauce ingredients:
¼ lb butter
1 apple (cored)
½ onion
1 banana
2 tablespoons mild to medium curry powder
100 ml white wine
600 ml fish stock
100 ml whipping cream
flour
clarified butter

Process:

Making the Curry Sauce

1. Sauté butter, apple, onion and banana.
2. In a pot, mix curry powder, fish stock and white wine and boil for ½ hour.
4. Puree everything together and add whipping cream.
5. Add salt and pepper to taste.

Scallops

1. Season scallops with salt and pepper
2. Dredge in flour, shaking off excess
3. Sauté in clarified butter
4. Arrange on curry sauce and garnish with diced banana
5. Serve with Basmati rice

Wine Suggestion:

American spice can be quite nice, when presented in Muscat form.
With grapefruit and lemon—a great bouquet—a match for seasoned scallops any day!
Now, curry and butter put forth their flavour.
The wine's spice wins with favour.
It complements the banana so fruity, with the great rice,
it does its duty!

Domaine de Grand Pre New York Muscat

Chef Jacques Poulin
Auberge au Lion D'or[66]

Baladin De Confit De Canard Du Lac Brome

Ingredients:

Baladin

6 duck legs
2 empire apples (diced)
3 tablespoons maple syrup
1 pack filo pastry

Vegetables

12 slices of apples
6 tablespoons maple syrup
braised red cabbage (to taste)

Sauce

½ cup veal stock
3¼ oz (90 gm) diced apples
one-third cup Cep D'Argent 'Mistral' liqueur
lemon juice (to taste)

Process:

1. Choose the four best duck legs (thighs) and cut at the joint.
2. De-bone the top parts of the legs as well as the remaining two duck legs in order to make the Napoleon Stuffing.
3. Caramelize the diced apples with maple syrup and add ½ of it to the mixture leaving ½ for the sauce.
4. Mix or blend.
5. Butter the filo pastry and cut to size in circular sheets (three sheets per serving; you can use a plate 10 inches in diameter).
6. Lay each serving of 3 buttered pastry sheets flat on a baking board one on top of the other.
7. In the centre of each pastry portion surround a duck leg 'bone end up' with the

Napoleon Stuffing.
8. Pat the stuffing around the leg so that it is firm.
9. Wrap the pastry around the stuffing and leg so that it is snug.
10. Bake all four portions at 350° F for 12 to 15 minutes.
11. Caramelize the 12 slices of apples with maple syrup.
12. Braise cabbage.
13. Serve each portion of duck with 3 slices of caramelized apples and braised cabbage with the sauce made up of the other half of the diced caramelized apples and Mistral liqueur.

Wine Suggestion:

> Le Canard enjoys his stature!
> Though it's only his legs here that matter!
> With apples and cabbage with sweetness galore!
> A special wine is needed all the more!
> To match all flavours complex. T'is hard to vex!
> Two vins come forward—one red and one white, but both that will please with delight!
> With plums and cherries the red is dry to contrast the sweet succulent bird.
> The white with bubbles so pleasing the eye. A flavour of citrus enhances—oh my!

Cep D'Argent 'La Reserve des Chevaliers' or Cep D'Argent 'Selection de Mousquetaires'

Chef Martin Polidano
Fazio's Restaurant

'Ricotta Gnocchi with Proscuitto and Herbs'

Ingredients:

4 gnocchi
250 g. ricotta
1 egg
¼ cup flour
salt to taste
boiling water

'Proscuitto and Herb Sauce'

Ingredients:

6 oz proscuitto diced
2 cloves garlic
2 scallions diced
basil, flat leaf parsley, chopped
olive oil
salt and pepper
Parmigianno Regiano
white wine
stock

Process:

Gnocchi

1. Place ricotta on working table and form a well.
2. Put ¼ cup flour, egg and salt in centre of well and blend.
3. Additional flour may be required depending on type of ricotta
4. Knead mixture into a ball.
5. Cut gnocchi into quarters and roll on a floured surface into long strips.
6. Cut gnocchi in ¼ inch segments and boil in salt water.

Process:

Sauce

1. In a large skillet add olive oil. When proper temperature (boiling/sizzling) is reached add proscuitto, garlic and scallions, sauté until slightly transparent. At this point, add white wine and stock.
2. When liquid returns to a boil, add cooked gnocchi and reduce until the sauce is creamy (not watery).
3. Add chopped herbs and Parmigiano Reggiano and serve.

Wine Suggestion:

The herb and spice combines well with the pleasant dryness of white wine.

Creekside Estate Winery Sauvignon Blanc

'Osso Bucco'

Ingredients (serves 4):

4 veal shanks varying in sizes between 12 and 20 ounces
1 large onion
6 cloves of garlic
flour
salt and pepper
1 bottle dry red wine
fresh rosemary
olive oil
brining liquid
½ lemon
20 black peppercorns

Process:

1. Prepare the brining liquid. Boil 4 cups of water with salt to taste. Add 20 black peppercorns, 2 bay leaves, 1 cup red wine and the juice extracted from ½ a lemon. Bring to boil and simmer for 5 minutes. Allow liquid to cool completely and then pour contents of liquid over osso buccos (veal shanks). Brine for 1 hour to a maximum of 24 hours. (This process will give your osso bucco a flavour boost from the inside and will work its way out).

2. The next step is to seal the osso bucco. Remove the osso bucco from the brine. Pat dry. Make slight cuts down the sides of the veal shanks (osso bucco). This will keep the shank from buckling under the extreme heat. Pour olive oil in sauté pan and allow pre-heating. At the same time, dredge osso bucco in flour and season liberally with salt and pepper. Place meat in hot pan and sear (2-3minutes each side) then place in a brazing oven dish.

3. In a separate pan, sauté 6 cloves of garlic, with large diced onion. After the onions turn opaque, add rosemary. After achieving a roasted colour, add remaining wine and demi-glace.[68] Reduce slightly and remove from heat. Pour contents of sauce over the meat, reserving 2 cups for final dishing. With the sauce over the osso

bucco, thin out with water to a consistency of a light jus.

4. Pre-heat oven to 375° F. Braise covered for 2 hours. Do not let dish braise in a dry state. Add liquid if necessary. Check periodically.

5. Pre-heat reserved sauce. You may wish to remove garlic pieces and add braising juices to enhance flavours.

Wine Suggestion:

This is an Italian, full flavoured delicacy. Veal with juices, garlic and red wine abound. Pour an exceptional red wine full of flavour, tasting of berries with pepper and spice that will send your taste buds souring!

Maleta Estate Winery Meritage

Chef Christopher Ennew C.C.C.
Ste. Anne's Country Inn and Spa

'Marinated Grilled Flank Steak'

Ingredients:

1 flank steak
4 cloves of garlic (fresh)
Dijon mustard
cracked black pepper
thyme

Process:

1. Crush the garlic and rub all over the steak.
2. Coat the steak with Dijon Mustard on all surfaces.
3. Season with the pepper.
4. Sprinkle with thyme.
5. Place the steak in a bag and let marinade in the fridge for at least 4 hours.
6. Grill on high heat turning once, cook to medium rare.
7. Slice the meat on the Bias, across the grain.

Note: It is imperative to let flank steak rest loosely before carving.
Cover with tin foil for 10 minutes so the steak will retain the juices.

Wine Suggestion:

The Chef, being so sincere, suggests that this meal be consumed with beer. If a wine should be needed,
let it be a great one that's heeded!

Stratus Red

Ste. Anne's Braised Lamb Shanks

Ingredients (serves 4):

4 lamb shanks
2 cups sliced carrots
2 cups pearl onions or chopped white onions
1 cup sliced celery
2 cups sliced mushrooms
2 bay leaves
2 cup red wine
2 cups beef broth
2 sprigs fresh rosemary
2 tablespoons thyme
salt and pepper to taste

Process:

1. Dredge shanks in flour. In a heavy pot, brown shanks in oil until all sides are evenly browned.
2. Remove shanks from pot and reserve.
3. Add chopped vegetables and sauté.
4. Add wine and stock and herbs, return shanks to pot and add enough water to cover shanks. Bring to a boil.
5. Reduce to simmer and cook covered for 1½ to 2 hours depending on the size of the shanks or until the meat has pulled away from the bone and is very tender.
6. Serve with garlic mashed potatoes.

Wine Suggestion:

> *Ba, ba, black sheep. A red wine is needed to feel full. This is a meal where a red wine will rule!*

Jackson-Triggs Proprietor's Grand Reserve Meritage

Chef Bernard

Nice Bistro[69]

'Pains Berger'

Ingredients (serves 2-6 persons):

2 tablespoons olive oil
4-6 slices French bread
1 apple
4-6 slivers goat cheese
4-6 slivers black olives (de-pitted)
herbes de provence[70]

Process:

1. Preheat oven to 350°F.
2. Brush bread lightly with olive oil.
3. Core and slice apple in 4-6 pieces.
4. Brush apple slices lightly with olive oil.
5. Grill or pan fry apple slices lightly.
6. Place one apple slice and goat cheese on each slice of bread.
7. Sprinkle herbs and black olive slivers.
8. Place bread on cookie sheet and bake at 350°F for 10 to 15 minutes.

Wine Suggestion:

Delicious cheese, though strong, makes a Mediterranean flare with olives and bread and apple. A wine red or white, young and vibrant makes good company splendid.

Legends Estates Sauvignon Blanc or *Colio Estates CEV Gamay Noir*

Herb-Crusted Pork Loin with Apple-Garlic Glaze

Ingredients (serves 4 to 6):

1 ½-2 lb boneless pork loin
2 tsp butter, melted
1 tsp dried rosemary
1 tsp onion powder
½ tsp dried marjoram or sage
½ tsp dried oregano
½ tsp salt
1/4 tsp black pepper
1/4 cup apple juice or white wine
1 ½ cups apple juice
4-6 cloves garlic, peeled and left whole

Process:

1. Pre-heat oven to 450°F.
2. Trim most of the visible fat from the pork. Rub melted butter over the pork loin. In a shallow dish, mix together herbs, salt and pepper.
3. Place pork loin face down in the herb mixture, pressing it in well. Turning pork over, coat with the rest of the spices.
4. Place in a shallow roasting pan, and roast uncovered for 20-30 minutes, turning pork to brown well on all sides.
5. Reduce heat to 325°F. Pour apple juice into pan, cover with foil. Continue to roast until pork is done and very tender. Remove from the oven and allow to rest (still covered) for 5-10 minutes.

Glaze:
Pour 1 ½ cups apple juice and the pan juices into a heavy bottom saucepan. garlic cloves and bring to a boil. Reduce to a simmer for 30-40 minutes, u
- 3/4 of a cup remains. Strain and serve with pork.

Wine Suggestion:

A loin so light and tender thus requires a wine of equal splendour—a wine of reddish colour, with a touch of lightness. A bit of strawberry/cranberry adds to the brightness. They meld with the fruit, the garlic and the juice. What flavours this wine turns loose!

Lotusland Pinot Noir or *Grand Pre Leon Millot*

Braised Harvest Vegetable Medley

This is a great dish to accompany your favourite roast on a cold day.

Ingredients (serves 6):

1 lb baby potatoes, halved
2 sweet potatoes, peeled and cut in bite size
3 parsnips, peeled and cut bite size
5 carrots, peeled and cut bite size
1 medium onion, chopped
1 tbsp butter
1/4 cup chicken stock
2 garlic cloves, minced
1 tsp dry thyme
½ tsp dry tarragon
½ tsp salt
1/8 tsp black pepper

Process:

1. Place potatoes, sweet potatoes, parsnips and carrots in greased 9 x 13 inch baking pan or shallow casserole dish.
2. Add onion and mix.
3. Bring chicken stock and butter to a boil. Stir in remaining ingredients. Pour mixture over vegetables. Toss gently.
4. Cover tightly with foil or lid. Bake at 400° F for 1 hour until vegetables are tender. Uncover for the last 10 to 15 minutes to evaporate some of the liquid in the pan.

Wine Suggestion:

> *Alone it requires a white wine with herbal measure. But with a roast, an elegant red, one will treasure.*

With a roast try *Gaspereau Vineyards Lucie Kuhlman.*[72] Or by itself, choose *L'Acadie Blanc from Blomidon Ridge.*

Chef Gabriella Occhiuto
Alta Rossa Restaurant[73]

Veal Shanks a la Rossa

Ingredients (serves 6):

6 12oz veal shanks
1 cup flour
¼ lb butter
3 tbsp olive oil
2 celery stalks, diced
2 large carrots, diced
6 whole plum tomatoes, diced
3 garlic cloves, finely chopped
3 large shallots, finely diced
16 oz fresh veal stock
¼ cup porcini mushrooms, rinsed
¼ cup mushrooms
1 small onion, diced
1 tbsp tomato paste
½ cup red wine
½ cup dry sherry
1 sprig fresh rosemary
1 sprig fresh marjoram
3 sprigs fresh parsley
12 leaves fresh basil
salt and pepper to taste

Process:

1. Dice tomato in small bite size chunks.
2. Finely chop and add all the fresh herbs to the tomato and set aside.
3. Place porcini mushrooms in a small bowl with 1 cup lukewarm water.
4. Rub salt and pepper onto veal shanks and dredge into flour, lightly coating both sides.
5. Place in hot frying pan and sear both sides of the veal shank until they are lightly browned.
6. Remove shanks and place in a deep roasting pan.
7. In a fry pan, add onion, shallots, carrots and celery.

8. Sauté until the onions become translucent.
9. Add the tomato paste and stir until vegetables are coated.
10. Deglaze the fry pan with wine and sherry and reduce liquid to ½.
11. Add veal stock and mushrooms and tomato mixture.
12. Simmer for 5 minutes.
13. Add salt and pepper to taste.
14. Combine all ingredients in roasting pan.
15. Cover roasting pan and cook slowly for two hours at 375° F or until tender.

Wine Suggestion:

A meal so divine requires a first among wine—one that exhibits quality so rare, why not try a wine whose grapes are dried in the air? The meal with protein and spice galore, must have a match with vanilla, cloves and berries to score!

Magnotta Enotrium[74] *V.Q.A.*

Whole Wheat Pasta e Fagioli with Saffron

Ingredients (serves 6):

1 package whole wheat ditali
2 stalks celery finely chopped in cubes
2 bulbs shallots finely chopped
3 garlic cloves finely chopped
2 19oz cans Romano beans (including liquid)
1 19 oz white kidney beans (including liquid)
¼ cup extra virgin olive oil
1 pinch saffron
½ lb pancetta sliced 1/8 inch thick, cut into cubes
salt and pepper to taste
3 cups chicken or vegetable stock
water
A drizzle of white truffle oil to finish plate if desired
shavings of fresh Parmiggiano Reggiano cheese

Process:

1. Place large soup pot on stove.
2. Add oil and onions.
3. When the onions become transparent, toss in the pancetta and celery.
4. When the pancetta becomes crisp, add the garlic and shallots. Continue to stir until garlic is slightly brown.
5. Add the stock and the saffron allowing the soup to come to a simmering boil.
6. Add Romano beans to the liquid.
7. Mash white kidney beans including liquid into a blender until creamy.
8. Pour mixture into the soup and continue to simmer for ½ hour.
9. Salt and pepper to taste.
10. Boil off whole wheat ditali as instructed on the package.
11. Drain off and add to the soup.
12. Garnish with shavings of Parmiggiano Reggiano.
13. For special occasions, you may finish the dish by drizzling white truffle oil or a good quality extra virgin olive oil.

Wine Suggestion:

Hearty, rustic—all in one meal! What kind of wine would fulfill this deal? A soup with beans, vegetables, garlic and more, such a wide taste each has in store. The wine need be diverse to pour. One with power and complex flavours to make tastes soar!

Magnotta Toro Nero

Greg Muscat[75]

Ross Fil-Forn (Baked rice)[76]

Ingredients:

1 pound of hamburger meat (medium)
1 Spanish onion
1 can of Bravo Spaghetti sauce
1 can of minced tomatoes
1 cup of grated cheddar cheese
½ cup of grated Parmesan cheese
2 eggs
1 cup of converted rice (white)
salt and pepper
Italian seasoning

Process:

1. Fry the hamburger and separate the grease from the meat.
2. Cut the onion up into ¼ inch cubes and fry over low heat.
3. Blend the meat and onion to gather and add the spaghetti sauce and the minced tomatoes.
4. Let simmer on low heat.
5. Boil the rice until it is half cooked.
6. Drain the rice and combine meat, onion and sauce mixture.
7. Beat 2 eggs and blind them in the sauce.
8. Add salt, pepper and Italian seasoning (to taste).
9. Pour the whole mixture into a large greased baking dish.
10. Blend in the two cheeses.
11. Bake at 350° F for about 30 to 45 minutes (until all liquid is absorbed) and a soft crust forms on top.

Wine Suggestion:

With rice almost any wine goes, but with tomato sauce and cheese of strength, a red wine will do fine!

Malivoire Lady Bug Rose

Desserts

Those Fabulous Desserts

Desserts have been left out in the cold—so to speak. There are many wives tales about wine and chocolate. Read on.

Wine and Chocolate

Wine and chocolate! There must be some mistake here? Wine and chocolate are worlds apart, n'est-ce pas? Not so.

According to the Coco Berry Institute, a leader in chocolate research and development, the cocoa tree arrived in Mexico just prior to the seventh century A.D. It was cultivated by the Mayas, Aztecs and Toltecs. The cocoa bean became food, currency, and had spiritual ties with the gods. Like wine, it was initially offered as a drink. Explorer Colombus rejected it. Conquistador Cortez welcomed it, and Spain encompassed it.

There is more to the common association between wine and chocolate than 'romance and love' and Valentine's Day. Both are the result of a plant product—wine from the vine and chocolate from the cocoa bean. Both have been cultivated for centuries. Wine dates back to Mesopotamia (or even further) and chocolate (or at least the cocoa tree) is recorded near the time of Christ. Both go through a fermentation process. There are countless varieties and styles of wine and chocolate. Both have similar storing temperatures. Both are noted for health benefits (in moderation). There are even vintage chocolates to go along vintage wines!

Chocolate, with its multitude of types and flavours, is ascending to the forefront of food and beverage pairings. Chocolatiers across Canada have their preferences when it comes to the dynamic duo.

Fess Parker, television's 'Daniel Boone' and 'Davy Crockett' is a noted chocolate and wine lover. In 1986, Fess launched his Double Tree Resort in Santa Barbara. One year later, he opened Fess Parker's Winery & Vineyard. Then he established the Wine Country Inn & Spa, Los Olivos in 1998.

Rodney's Single Vineyard Syrah with dark chocolate truffles dusted with bittersweet cocoa, both ingredients picking up on the chocolate notes in the wine and enhancing its intense jam and berry quality. He enjoys that pairing on special holidays with his family. Fess also loves peanut brittle and tawny port.

I had the privilege of speaking with Dominique and Cindy Duby about the subject of wine and chocolate at their Vancouver-based international consulting and creative firm and when they were in Toronto at a special seminar they hosted (in collaboration with Donald Ziraldo of Inniskillin Winery) about wine and chocolate pairings. Dominique and Cindy specialize in food and wine concepts. They are world-acclaimed patissiers, chocolatiers and writers of 'Wild Sweets—Exotic Dessert & Wine pairings'. They trained under master pastry chefs such as Lenotre Paris and Wittamer in Brussels, and they are winners of many gold and silver medals (including the World Pastry Cup, France). "We think that one of the best, if not the best pairing to Chocolate (dark) would have to be sweet fortified wines (i.e., Vintage Port—most aged fortified wines do not have high levels of tannins and thus are much better companions to chocolate. White chocolate, on the other end, especially when mixed with fruits, works very well with icewine, and that is one of our favourites."

Donald Ziraldo, co-founder of Inniskillin Wines in Niagara recently asked Dominique and Cindy to create a sensory, gastronomic treat by merging four Inniskillin Icewines with chocolate.

Edmonton's, Dennis Yurkiwsky, who studied under Toronto based French Master, Jean Yves Vendeville, established 'Chocolate Exquisite' in 2002. Making high quality, European style (French) chocolates, Mr. Yurkiwsky recently succeeded in making the Chocolate Pysankyas or Ukrainian Easter Egg—a very great feat! A lover of high quality wine, he wrote in an email to me, "As far as my favourite wine with chocolate—my natural disposition is to have a fine cognac with the chocolate but I have been known to consume wine with it as well." According to Denis,

> Until recently, chocolate was basically categorized into 3 main groups (dark, milk and white) with some sub-categorizations to allow for the percentage of cocoa mass. So, one would choose their wine or beverage based upon the sweetness (% cocoa mass) of the chocolate.
>
> A recent innovation is the single origin chocolate, which is chocolate that is manufactured from a specific variety of bean grown in one region. Within a specific region you can find the best of the best, the ler cru[77] of the plantation.
>
> There is tremendous variety in the flavour of single origin chocolates because of the influence of the soil and growing conditions on the beans. While red wine has more than 500 identified flavour components, chocolate has over 1500. At recent chocolate tasting events, I have spoken on the topic of chocolate tasting, focusing on single origin and estate chocolate. I pair them with a number of dessert wines and port. Over the

many unforgettable chocolate and wine-filled experiments that I regularly conduct, my senses tell me that they have 15 favourite parings of wine with single origin chocolate (6 1er cru and 7 unique blends).

Jenn Stone, owner of *'js bon bons'* in Toronto knows about chocolate. She has gained a wealth of experience by working in the pastry kitchens of many top restaurants. She also studied at the Culinary Institute of America and the International School of Confectionary Arts. A very busy person—she's well on her way to opening up a chocolate making school. Jenn has this to say her about her tastes, "Pairing wine and chocolate can be very tricky because of the tannin involved. I prefer the complexity of 'Barolo Chinato' a multidimensional digestive made from 24 herbs and spices added to slightly sweetened Barolo wine. Its flavours make it ideal for chocolate—as well as being delicious on its own as an aperitif. My other two choices would be 'Kriek', a cherry beer with a distinctive taste made in Belgium. For white and lighter chocolate, I would suggest a Brussels White Beer again from Belgium." Nice stuff—sounds yummically delicious!

Beer master at Magnotta winery, Michael Ligas favours Porter and/or Stout with his chocolate. Magnotta product consultant, Cesar Valence prefers the delectable flavours of the Magnotta Framboise—a beverage that is almost like liqueur in nature and packed with raspberry aroma and taste.

With over one hundred and seventy years of family tradition as pastry chefs, bakers and chocolate makers, Willem Hellema, President of William's Chocolates in Whitby, Ontario loves his chocolates. "I'm not much of a drinker of alcoholic products but my advice to someone who wants to enjoy chocolate with something—or even have something around to offer with chocolate as a dessert, is to have a liqueur on hand such as Grand Marnier. The chocolate/fruit flavours will intermingle and complement each other."

Having discovered that chocolate makers are well-versed when it comes to pairing sweets with wine, I decided to find out what winemakers and wine writers have to say about the topic. Not surprisingly, they know what they like.

Irwin Smith of *Ocala Farm Orchards Winery* in Port Perry prefers fruit wines with his chocolate, even though he produces award winning grape wines. "I enjoy bitter sweet to mild sweet dark chocolate with my Ocala Raspberry and Ocala Black Currant wines," he says, "the chocolate tannin seems to meld with the fruit acid and flavours to produce a luscious effect."

Sandy and Fred Archibald of *Archibald Estates Farm Orchard Winery* suggest trying Canadian Maple, an apple/maple syrup wine that agrees with nutty and chocolate desserts and Royal Raspberry, an apple and raspberry wine this is ideal with Belgian truffles. Both wines are sweet dessert wines—Canadian Maple is the sweeter of the two.

Donald Triggs, President and CEO of Vincor International (also co-founder and President of Jackson-Triggs) had this to say, "For dry or semi-dry unsweetened chocolate my vote would be Delaine Vineyard Cabernet-Merlot (with its minty, raspberry, chocolate-vanilla flavours). For sweet chocolate, try Jackson-Triggs Cabernet Franc Icewine."

Daniel Pambianchi President and General Manager of Cadenza Wines Inc. (and owner of Maleta Winery in Niagara) says his favourite wine for pairing with chocolate is, without a doubt, port wine with icewine as a close second. Our 2001 Maleta Vidal Icewine would be my pick. I prefer sweet chocolate over bitter darker chocolate."

Angel's Gate in Niagara seems a very appropriate place to be suggesting a pairing of wine with a cocoa product. Indeed, even Willy Wonka had a special place to celebrate chocolate. Angelic Natalie Spytkowski has what she considers a perfect match, Angel's Gate 2002 Single Vineyard Merlot with dark chocolate, what else!

Wine writer Alex Eberspaecher likes his port and dark chocolate whenever he needs a lift. On being a romantic on Valentine's Day, he replied, "I like the pairing (chocolate/wine) any time, so perhaps I'm overly romantic."

Tony Aspler loves dessert. "I have my chocolate desserts [his favourite is chocolate mousse] with either vintage port or sweet sherry, this combo is a dinner item."

Those attending Konzelmann Estates Winery will get an extra treat this February. Normally, they are presented with 'icewine' chocolate with icewine or mint truffles with merlot. However this time, Herbert Konzelmann has prepared a wine/chocolate match made in wine/chocolate heaven, chocolate covered coffee beans and Konzelmann Pinot Noir. The combined coffee and chocolate aromas and flavours meld nicely with the berry, cherry and subtle chocolate of the wine.

Most of us rely on outside assistance in the form or restaurants and dessert cafes to satiate our 'chocappetite'. 'Michaels Back Door' is the name of a stylish Italian restaurant in Mississauga. Manager Mario Della-Savia seems to know his matches well. "I love chocolate, how about this match," he says, responding to my inquiry. "Luscious chocolate mousse with a Ferreira Dona Antonia Personal Reserve Port." You could almost hear him salivating (maybe that was me?) Mario also suggested a California Murphy-Goode Cabernet with—are your ready—"nice light pastry balls drizzled with chocolate sauce on top of strawberries" or "chocolate fondue on fresh fruit along with an Italian Ceasari Amarone."

Anton Potvin, co-owner of 'The Niagara Street Café' recommends trying deep fried brownies along with a mainly (75%) Grenache-based fortified wine[78] from the Pyrenees in southwest France. While I asked him about chocolate, he was quick to point out another one of his favourite matches—banana bread pudding and along with a Cave Spring, Indian-Summer Late Harvest wine. You will love it!

Finally, Rob Fracchioni, Executive Chef at the Millcroft Inn and Spa in Guelph has this selection. He told me the story about matching a wine to his creation: 'The Chocolate Espresso Tort'. "I couldn't find a wine to match up to this dessert. Almost everything I tried was overpowered by it. So I went home and started uncorking bottles to match it. I came upon the perfect match: A 1998 Cabernet Sauvignon from Cave Spring Cellars. The wine was older so the tannins were more reserved and stood up to but didn't compete with the dessert." Great match!

The combinations and places to enjoy them are as varied as one's imagination. The fireplace and comfy couch with a special love still appeals as the best setting for this Valentine's Day. However, moderation in both wine and chocolate is the key. Learn a lesson from Aztec Chief Montezuma who drank 50 cups of liquid chocolate per day. Could that have been 'Montezuma's Revenge?'

ON TASTING CHOCOLATE AND WINE

Tasting wine and chocolate need not be difficult—even with dry wines. Here are a few simple tips on tasting both.

1. Pour a bit of wine (red or white depending on the chocolate being tasted) into a tulip shaped glass. Examine the wine's colour, clarity. Swirl it a bit to release its bouquet and aroma. Sniff lightly as not to overpower your nasal senses. Sip a bit. Roll it around your mouth exposing your tongue's sensors to the wine. Swallow and savour the aftertaste or finish.
2. Take a bit of water to cleanse your palate.
3. Now, take a bite of the chocolate. Chew the chocolate and roll it around your tongue—again take the time to savour the flavours. (Chocolatier, Willem Hellema says too many people bite and swallow too fast.)
4. Take another sip of the wine while you still have the chocolate in your mouth. Mingle the flavours and let them marry to each other.
5. Savour the beauty of the merged taste.

Matching the Chocolate to the Wine

There are many types and styles of chocolates. Former Olympic skater and present Vice-President of Marketing for Jackson-Triggs, Cathy Jacobs leads us on a tour through the wine/chocolate maize!

1. *Natural Vanilla Chocolate* has a creamy rich hazelnut, vanilla and creamy smell and silky texture. It matches well with a barrel-aged Chardonnay, with essences of toasted oak, nuts and citrus with a creamy butter finish. Try Jackson-Triggs Proprietor's Grande Reserve Chardonnay.
2. *Crunch Caramel Toffee* smells of creamed caramel and burnt sugar with a hint of coffee flavour and is crunchy in texture. It goes with a Bordeaux style premium wine with concentrated fruit flavours of berries, chocolate, coffee and firm but supple tannins. Pair it with Jackson-Triggs Proprietor's Grande Reserve Meritage.
3. *Chocolate that has extra creamy milk* with a butter cream and coconut smell; a caramel, tropical fruit (mangoes, pineapple) flavour; and a silky texture should be paired with a Pinot Noir that has cherry, blackberry, and vanilla augmented soft tannins such as a Delaine Vineyards Pinot Noir or try a Cabernet Franc Icewine.
4. *With chocolate having a 70% Cocoa Butter*[79] *content* and a soft smoke, almond/coffee smell, a butterscotch almond cocoa flavour and is slightly gritty in texture, one should try a Bordeaux style red wine with raspberry, plum, chocolate and vanilla flavours such as a Proprietor's Reserve (Black Label) Meritage.
5. *Chocolate with a content of 85% Cocoa Butter and* having roasted, baked brownie aromas, smooth texture with firm tannins, bitter sweet balanced flavours, one would best try a premium wine such as Grande Reserve Meritage.

Other Wine and Dessert Matches

When matching wine to dessert the wine should be as sweet as or sweeter than the dessert. This is the general rule of thumb. However, even a dry wine with similar characteristics as a sweet dessert may do very well.

Here are some of my 'signature' parings of wine-styles and desserts. Keep in mind that various dessert wines are suitable for each of the following desserts.

Bonnie Gordon Cakes

Three Coconut Cake

Ingredients (recipe makes 9" round)

1 ½ cups sugar
½ cup butter, softened
2 large eggs
1 large egg white
2-¼ cups all-purpose flour
2-½ teaspoons baking powder
½ teaspoon salt
1-¼ cups canned coconut milk
1 teaspoon pure Bourbon vanilla extract
¾ cup unsweetened flaked coconut toasted in a 350° F oven

Procedure:

1. Preheat oven to 350° F.
2. Beat granulated sugar and butter in a mixer (medium speed) until well blended (about 5 minutes). Add eggs and egg white, one at a time, beating well after each addition.
3. Whisk flour, baking powder and salt in a separate bowl.
4. Add the flour mixture and coconut milk to sugar mixture. Begin by adding the flour mixture and then add the coconut milk. Alternate adding flour and coconut, ending with the flour mixture.
5. Stir in vanilla extract and ¾ cup of toasted unsweetened coconut.
6. Pour batter into 2 prepared cake pans and bake for 30 minutes or until a toothpick inserted in center comes out clean.

Coconut Buttercream

Ingredients (makes 5 cups):

1-1/4 cups sugar
5 large egg whites
2 cups (4 sticks) unsalted butter, room temperature
1 teaspoon pure vanilla extract
1 cup unsweetened flaked coconut toasted
¼ cup coconut rum liqueur

Procedure:

1. Combine egg whites, sugar, and vanilla in a heatproof bowl of an electric mixer. Set bowl over a pan of simmering water. Whisk constantly until sugar has dissolved and whites are hot to the touch (5 to 7 minutes).
2. Transfer bowl to the electric mixer. Using whisk attachment, mix on low speed, gradually increasing to high speed, until stiff, glossy peaks form (about 10 minutes).
3. In a separate bowl, beat butter until creamy and fluffy.
4. At low speed, add butter to egg whites, mixing until smooth. Add vanilla, coconut rum liqueur and continue mixing until incorporated. Fold in coconut. Use immediately.

Wine suggestion:

Luscious and creamy sweet—a lovely treat. A luxurious match with wines of ice is hard to beat.

Ocala Vin de Glace or Inniskillin Sparkling Icewine

Apple Pie

Try apple pie with late harvest or icewines such as:

1. *D.D. Leobard Iced Strawberry*
2. *Inniskillin Riesling*
3. *Vidal Icewine*
4. *Legends Estates Icewine*

Ice-cream

Sparkling wines have always pleased ice-cream lovers. Try:

1. *Magnotta Cabernet Franc Sparkling Icewine*
2. *Inniskillin Sparkling Icewine*
3. *Archibald Orchards Canadian Maple, made from the finest Canadian maple syrup*
4. *Ontario/BC Late Harvest Vidal/Riesling—a dessert wine that is made from grapes picked very late in the season and approach icewine in sweetness but not price*
5. *Iced Apple or Framboise,*[80] *both sweet dessert wines*

Crème Brulee

1. *Fieldstone Fruit Wines Wild Black Cherry Dessert Wine*
2. *Reif Select Late Harvest Vidal*
3. *BC/Ontario Medium Dry Sparkling*

Nuts

I like port style wine with nuts. Try:

1. *Magnotta Port*
2. *Winegarden Estate Blackberry Liqueur*
3. *D.D. Leobard Blueberry Dessert Wine*

Tiramisu, Trifle, and Soufflés

1. *Cep D'Argent Le Fleuret*[81]
2. *Nova Scotian Muscat*
3. *Ontario Sparkling Icewine*

Meringues, Strawberry with Cream, and Chocolate Sauce

1. *Jackson-Triggs Cab Franc Icewine*
2. *Magnotta Moscato Superiore Sparkling*

Strawberries and Raspberries (unsweetened and/or no cream)

You can use wine as a sauce. Try pouring the following or similar wines over fruit:

1. *Burrowing Owl Cabernet Franc*
2. *Jackson-Triggs Grand Reserve Merlot*
3. *Maleta Meritage*
4. *Mission Hill Occulus*
5. *Orofino Vineyards Meritage*
6. *Osoyoos-Larose*
7. *Reif First Growth Merlot*
8. *Sumac Ridge Pinnacle*
9. *Unity*

DESCRIPTION OF WINERIES USED IN SPECIFIC FOOD MATCHES[82]

Ontario Wineries

Angels Gate Winery Winemaker: Natalie Spytkowsky
www.angelsgatewinery.com

Angels Gate is truly a perfect blend of the traditional and modern in both its architecture and its wines. Built in the style of a Spanish mission, the unique and beautiful winery building is situated at the Niagara Escarpment Bench amongst rows of vineyards, scenic ponds and a backdrop of wooded forest. Like many vineyards in France and Germany, this property once belonged to the Congregation of Missionary Sisters of Christian Charity.

Angels Gate has two vineyards, one adjacent to the winery (10 acres) and one some 5 kilometres away (25 acres). The winery also obtains grapes from other growers. Angels Gate wines have won many awards and accolades. Their wines reflect the experience and care given by the winemaking team—especially its winemaker, Natalie Sptkowsky who is a model of dedication and knowledge. She believes in the philosophy that 'Less is More'. The less you fool around with something—the more you get. Conversely, the more you tinker, the more are your chances of spoiling the product. The winemaking facilities are underground thus giving more control and preciseness in the winemaking.

The wonderful view of Lake Ontario, the restaurant, special events and the charming staff make Angels Gate a popular tourist destination.

Archibald Orchards and Estate Winery Winemaker: Fred Archibald
www.archibalds-estatewinery.on.ca

Growing up in Niagara's fruit belt and having the Director of Vineland's Horticultural Research Station (and Brights Wines Chemist) as a father obviously benefited Archibald Orchards and Estate owner Fred Archibald.

The winery has it roots as a producer of apples. At one time, the estate was a thriving 'pick your own' fruit business. It featured a farm market and play area. More recently, the owners added a nine hole, par three golf course with all the trimmings. In 1997, Fred and his wife Sandy established *Archibald Orchards and Estate Winery*. In addition to the other attractions, the staff regularly organizes popular events throughout the year.

The estate produces fruit wines that hold true to Fred's philosophy—wine should taste like the fruit it is made from. Wine experts call them 'the best fruit wine in Ontario.' The winery sports a vast variety of apple, apple-fruit blends, fruit and dessert wines—excellent wines for many types of occasions.

Cave Spring Cellars Winemaker: Angelo Pavan
www.cavespring.ca

Cave Spring Cellars is situated in historic Jordan, Ontario; a region that has a rich heritage. The caves that hold the springs contain native Canadian artifacts. The Mississauga Indians inhabited the area in the late 1700's.

Cave Spring Cellars is a popular tourist haven consisting of the Cave Spring Cellars Winery (on the site of former Jordan Wine Co.), On The Twenty Restaurant, Inn on the Twenty, and a myriad of shops. Owner Len Pennechetti (he was the one who built the Cellars), brother Tom, and partner/winemaker Angelo Pavan, have realized their vision of providing high calibre food and service, and the Inn is decadent in its richness and comfort. Equally impressive are the wines they create, such as Riesling, Cabernet and Gamay Noir Reserve.

Cave Springs Vineyard, planted in 1978, is located on the Niagara Escarpment and is one of Niagara's oldest vineyards. Its proximity to Lake Ontario, heavy clay soil and hillside location makes it an ideal spot for growing grapes.

Angelo credits much of the success to the fine location of Cave Springs' vineyards on the Niagara Escarpment Bench. Here the airflow protects the vines from the harsh winter winds and spring frosts and moderates the very hot summers.

Chateau des Charmes Winemakers: Paul M. Bosc and Anna Maruggi
www.chateaudescharmes.com

Educated at the University of Burgundy winemaking school in Dijon, France and descended from a long line of winemakers from Algeria and Alsace, Paul Bosc Sr. was the first to plant vineyards completely consisting of vinifera[83] grapes in Canada. Paul Bosc Sr. is regarded as one of the major pioneers in developing total vinifera vineyards. He is also the first to produce single vineyard wines from grapes grown, vinified and bottled at the estate. The wines are excellent especially those from the Paul Bosc Estate and St. David's Estate single vineyards.

Colio Estates Winery Winemaker: Carlo Negri
www.coliowines.com

In 1980, Italian winemaker, Carlo Negri came to Ontario with the intent of growing vines and making fine wines. That year, he opened Colio Estates Winery in the Lake Erie North Shore near a town called Harrow. He chose this area because it is on the same latitude as Tuscany in Italy and Northern California. This area also has one of the longest growing seasons in Canada.

Referred to as the most southern winery in Canada, Colio makes fine red wines that can be classed as being 'avante garde'. Owning over 200 acres in the region, the winery sports some 500 French, American and European oak barrels in a large, humidity controlled cellar.

Carlo takes pride in his ultra premium (CVE) and premium (CV) red and white wines. Celebrating the 25th anniversary of great winemaking gives him every right to be proud!

Creekside Estates Winery Winemakers: Craig McDonald, Rob Power
www.creeksidewine.com

Located near Jordan Station and on 16 Mile Creek, this relatively new winery is producing first class wines such as a lovely Sauvignon Blanc. The winery is a picturesque place to visit. It features nature trails, picnic areas, a very large (400) barrel cellar and tasting room. The owners (Peter and Laura McCain Jensen) also have holdings in the Annapolis Valley, Nova Scotia (Blomindon Estate Winery, Lookoff Estate) as well as in St. Davids near Niagara-on-the-Lake.

Crown Bench Estates Winery Winemaker: Peter Kocsis
www.crownbenchestates.com

Crown Bench is one of the most promising wineries in Canada. It is situated on the crest of the Niagara Escarpment with he Bruce Trail running some 100 metres behind the winery. The view from the vineyard of Lake Ontario and the Toronto Skyline is spectacular. Huge megalithic rock decorations give the Estate the appearance of a prehistoric temple.

Crown Bench wines are as spectacular as the location. The reds are highly concentrated and balanced. The whites, especially the Chardonnays, can compete with the best in the world. The Grape Growers of Ontario crowned co-owner, Livia Sipos as the 2004 Grower of the Year.

D'Angelo Estates Winery Winemaker: Sal D'Angelo

www.dangelowinery.com

In 1984, Sal D'Angelo purchased some 50 acres of land in Amherstburg, just south of Windsor, Ontario. Since his first vintage in 1989, he has won over 60 awards and medals including Ontario's 'Best Dessert Wine' two years in a row. Having one of the foremost wineries in Ontario is not enough. Sal has turned his attention to the Okanagan Valley, more specifically, to the Naramata Bench where he purchased seven acres and is planning to buy another twenty-two acres. The first vintage from his Okanagan winery was produced in 2005.[84]

Henry of Pelham Family Estate Winery Winemaker: Ron Giesbrecht

www.henryofpelham.com

Historic Henry of Pelham has roots that go back some 220 years. Owned and operated by the Speck family since 1988, the land was first deeded to their great, great, great grandfather in 1794 after having served as a fifer in 'Butlers Rangers'. Gravestones on the property still mark the burial spots of Mr. Smith, his wife and members of his family.

The wines of Henry of Pelham have always been described as consistent, powerful, concentrated, long lasting and elegant. The winemaker has been deemed a treasure by many wine critics. The public can tour the winery, taste wines, picnic on the grounds or enjoy light meals at the Coach House Café.

Known for its powerful Cabernets and Merlot, Henry of Pelham almost single handedly saved the Baco Noir grape from almost certain demise and restored its prominence in the early 1990's.

Inniskillin Wines Winemakers: Karl Kaiser and James Manners

www.inniskillin.com

Colonel Cooper served in the War of 1812 as a solider in an Irish Regiment called the 'Inniskilling Fusiliers'.[85] For his service, he was granted Crown land, which he called Inniskillin Farm. In 1975, taking the name from the early heritage of the region, Karl J. Kaiser and Donald J.P. Ziraldo incorporated Inniskillin Wines. They were the first to receive a license to operate a winery since 1929. Until then, the wines that were produced in Ontario and the rest of Canada were largely inferior. Ziraldo (an Agriculturist educated at Guelph University) and Kaiser (a Chemistry graduate from Brock University) started with a vision of producing premium quality wines from vinifera vines grown in the Niagara Peninsula. Many had their doubts, but the result was beyond expectation. In 1978, a Burgundian shipper, Chauvenet ordered 600 cases of Inniskillin Marachel Foch.[86]

By 1991, Inniskillin Icewine brought Canada to the forefront by winning top awards at Vin Expo, a prestigious wine competition in Bordeaux. The reputation of the winery, and its co-founders, was set in stone. They maintain that tradition today with the addition of Australian winemaker, James Manners.

Inniskillin, now part of the Vincor family of wines,[87] has achieved world prominence and is highly regarded for all its high quality wines. As a millennium project, Inniskillin commissioned renowned architect Bruno Freschi to design a building to celebrate the style of Frank Lloyd Wright. The Brae Burn Barn in which the boutique is located is reputed to have been designed or influenced by Frank Lloyd Wright himself.

Donald Ziraldo has become world famous for his passionate promotion of Canadian wines. "Wherever I am in the world, my heart is never far from Inniskillin."

Jackson-Triggs Niagara Estate Winery

Winemakers: Tom Seaver and Kristine Casey

www.jacksontriggswinery.com

Co-founders Donald Triggs (Marketer) and Alan Jackson (Chemist) established Jackson-Triggs Vintners in 1993. Jackson-Triggs is another member of Vincor. The winery had its Grand Opening on July 26, 2001. It is regarded by many as a state-of-the-art winery with superb grounds, gardens, Greek amphitheatre and vineyards. The winery, designed to optimize quality and environmental friendliness, was inspired by traditional farm buildings but was built using high-tech construction. The winemaking facilities employ the most advanced equipment from all over globe.

Jackson-Triggs wines have proven themselves at all levels of world competition. With titles such as 'Chardonnay du Monde' (Burgundy), Best of Nation (Canada), Best Canadian Producer (International Wine and Spirits Competition awarded in England), and Concours Mondial de Bruxelles Great Gold (Belgium), these wines are living proof of the premium quality of Canadian wines.

However, Donald and is wife, Elaine have collaborated on another venture to obtain the best possible grapes for Jackson-Triggs. They bought some 100 acres of prized fruit land adjacent to the Niagara Parkway in 1998 and named it Delaine Vineyards, which is a combination of their first names.

The Triggs' are meticulous in their treatment of their vineyard, which is kept in impeccable shape ensuring that Delaine serves as a research facility to maximize fruit quality. Delaine is their personal vineyard that has been spared no expense from the cultivating methods (different clones of same species are grown to experiment with blends and soils) to the large air circulators placed in the vineyards to help the air flow over the vines when the temperature falls below a certain degree.

The wines, first released in 2001, have been called premium wines made by premium winemakers Tom Seaver (B.Sc., Oenology/Food Science, Cal-State University; Chief Winemaker) and Kristine Casy (B.Sc. Brock University, CCOVI Program).[88]

Kacaba Vineyards Winemaker: Beth Mischuk
www.kacaba.com

Kacaba is a relatively new family owned winery located on the Niagara Escarpment Bench. They are producing wines that can only be described as 'avante garde'. The premium wines are made for long ageing (the Merlot is as good as gold as well as the Cabernet Sauvignon, Reserve, Shiraz and Meritage). Kacaba had one of the first functional plantings of Shiraz in Niagara.

The winery grounds are very scenic and are continually being improved. It is amazing that at one time, just before purchase, this property was slated to become a subdivision. That would have been tragic since there is a growing demand for Kacaba wines. The owners wish to keep quantities small and quality ultra premium. However, there will be pressure to expand.

Konzelmann Estate Winery Winemakers: Herbert Konzelmann, Matthias Boss
www.konzelmannwines.com

Winemaker and owner Herbert Konzelmann has been producing wine since 1984. He comes from generations of winemakers—the family has operated a winery in Germany since 1893.

Konzelmann wines are known for their Germanic style and harmony of fruit flavours. His Riesling and Chardonnay wines are exceptional. The Konzelmann Merlot Grande Reserve Classic, Cabernet-Merlot Reserve (unfiltered) are awesome in their character with blackberry jam, earth and oak integrated with pepper, vanilla and berry fruit flavours—very complex and they becomes more complex as they age with evolving flavours.

The main attraction of the Konzelmann estate, however, is meeting Herbert himself. A fine gentleman by any standards, there is always a smile and a kind word. With plans to build a new winery under way, his smile is getting bigger.

Legends Estates Winery Winemaker: Paul Lizak
www.LegendsEstates.com

Legends Estates was originally a fruit farm planted in 1946 by the present owner's grandfather, John Lizak. Fruit from the 200 acre farm was initially sold to other wineries. However, Paul soon realized that he too could make wine from his quality grapes.

From his first vintage in 2000, it was apparent that Legends Estates wines were marked for greatness winning gold, silver and gold medals in national and international competition. The wall street journal rated Legends Estates Icewines as having the best taste and value.
Legends, produces many fine wines. I am personally extremely fond of their Pinot Noir Reserve and Sauvignon Blanc.

Longdog Winery Winemaker: James Lahti
www.longdog.ca

What happens when the 'Call of the Country' takes over the mind of a city dweller? Here's the story of one such case.

In 1997, TV/Film Editor and Producer James Lahtl and wife Victoria Rose were urged by close friend Steve Rapkin to purchase a 'private getaway'—a sort of country retreat. The three of them ended up in Prince Edward County, just outside the town of Milford at a 300-acre property, which sported a 160 year old farmhouse. They bought it on the spot!

The 'weekend getaway' soon became a permanent business address and they turned the farm property into vineyard two years later. They initially planted 1,200 vines of Chardonnay, Pinot Noir, Pinot Blanc and Gamay. If this reminds you of Burgundy, you're correct since the soils and climate are similar to that great wine producing area. By 2003, they had almost 20,000 vines planted—three original varieties plus the addition of Pinot Grigio.

By May of 2004, they began selling their wines. They were a big hit.

Magnotta Estates Winery Winemakers: Marco Zamunerand and Peter Rotar
www.magnotta.com

This award winning winery has over 2,200 international, national and prestigious awards. It has something for everyone whether gourmet, browser, wine novice or connoisseur. The large (75,000 square foot) flagship[89] winery in Vaughan has an impressive cathedral ceiling and collection of Group of Seven paintings, sculptures and other art. It is home to a wide variety of wines representing the best of Ontario and Product of Canada wines. The Beamsville location offers wine tasting, tours and an art collection that features Niagara's artists.

Gabe and Rossana Magnotta have carved out a piece of Canadian wine history by realizing their dream of a winery that has national and international recognition. Superb wines for discriminating palates!

Malivoire Wine Company Winemaker: Ann Sperling
www.malivoirewineco.com

Opening in 1999, this winery quickly rose to prominence with its innovative winery and wines. Winemaker, Ann grew up in the Okanagan Valley where she gained much experience working for Andres, Cedar Creek, Cilento and Creekside and other wineries before coming to Malivoire.

Situated on the Beamsville Bench, the estate is comprised of three vineyard properties: the Moira Vineyard where Chardonnay and Pinot Noir is grown; the Estate Vineyard, where the winery is located, grows Pinot Noir, Chardonnay, Pinot Gris, Gewürztraminer, Melon and Chardonnay Musque; and the Old Vines Foch Vineyard located in Jordan where chardonnay, Pinot Gris, Cabernet Franc and Gamay are grown.

Nothing artificial or synthetic touches the soil or vines. No chemical insecticides, herbicides or fertilizers are used. Everything is strictly organic.

Recently, Malivoire is experimenting with Stelvin®, Screw-Cap Closures. Ann Sperling says, "Extensive quality research indicates that aging is more controlled and measured in wines closed with screw caps than the same wines closed with traditional corks.' To date, Stelvin® uses screw caps on all of their bottles except for two wines.

Proprietor, Martin Malivoire is keen to explore any option that will improve his vineyards and wines. If the concentration and flavour of these wines is any indication, I say, "explore!"

Maleta Estate Winery Winemaker: Stan Maleta and Daniel Pambianchi
www.maletawinery.com

Stan and Marilyn Maleta started Maleta Estate Winery in 1998, on the site of what is thought to be the oldest commercial winery in Niagara (circa early 1800's) and also the site of Sunnieholme Winery, which existed there in 1918.

Stan was obsessed with making first rate Bordeaux-style reds. Daniel Pambianchi teamed up with Stan to produce premium and ultra-premium wines. Daniel is a successful amateur winemaker, writer (*Techniques in Home Winemaking: A Practical Guide to Making Chateau Style Wines* and contributing author and technical editor for *Winemaker Magazine*) and telecom-engineer.

The team flourished and produced such world class wines as a Meritage (a blend of Cabernet Sauvignon, Merlot and Cabernet Franc mix) and a Cabernet-Merlot blend (60-40). Also, their Gamay Noir is an experience of fruit tastes.

Cadenza Wines Inc. now owns Maleta Wines, but remains under the Maleta company name. Daniel Pambianchi is President and General Manager. His small winery will continue to produce big wines.

Niagara College Teaching Winery Winemakers: Jim Warren and Jordan Harris
www.nctwinery.com

Niagara College Teaching Winery (NCT) not only teaches students about wine, they also make award-wining wine. Winemaker, Jim Warren has become something of a legend in the Ontario wine industry having established himself as a top amateur before founding Stoney Ridge Cellars. He is a heavily sought after consultant.

NCT is first and foremost a place that prepares students for employment in the wine industry. Experimental vineyards such as the Jack Forrer Vineyard enable them to experience the variables important to growing grapes and growing top quality fruit, which goes into the making of NCT wines.

NCT makes several excellent wines including Pinot Noir, Warren Classic Chardonnay, Cabernet Sauvignon, and Meritage.

Ocala Orchards Farm Winery Winemaker: Irwin Smith
www.ocalawinery.com

Not many people took Irwin Smith seriously when, in 1992, he announced his intentions to sell his music business and plant vines on his family's orchard located between Whitby and Port Perry, Ontario. The 100-acre farm was purchased by Irwin's grandfather in 1915 and was used to raise cattle. In 1978, the cattle farm was slowly converted into an apple orchard.

In 1995, Irwin opened up the Ocala Winery—and proved all his doubters wrong. Using a technique that buries the vines to prevent frost damage (used by Quebec viticulturists), he was able to grow vinifera and viniferal hybrid vines that have produced prize-winning wines. In addition, he produces first class fruit wines and is always experimenting with blends. In 2000, many of his products earned the V.Q.A.

Irwin, ably assisted by wife, Alissia, produces some lovely Rieslings, luscious Vin de Glace (similar to an icewine) and interesting Chardonnays. If Irwin says he's going to tackle a vineyard in the North Pole—many will think twice before doubting him again.

Pelee Island Winery Winemakers: William Schmoranz, Martin Janz and Jeff Kah
www.peleeisland.com

Winery President and Winemaster, William Schmoranz, was born in Ruedesheim, Germany where he gained much of his winemaking experience. In 1985, he joined Pelee Island Winery. He is now ably assisted by Martin Janz (Rheingau Insitute of Winemaking, Germany) and Jeff Kah (Niagara College Oenology Program, Honours).

The history of winemaking in Pelee Island goes back to J.S. Hamilton in 1891. Since his pioneering efforts, the winery has become synonymous with producing quality wines and grapes and that have won many awards and accolades. The winery's vineyards, which cover some 500+ acres, are strictly cultivated with natural products according to the World Wildlife Fund's 'Strict Sustainable Vineyard Practice.' The winery's Chardonnay, Gewurtraminer, Reisling, Cabernets, Pinot Noirs and Tempranillo are very much in demand.

What makes Pelee Island both a great place for winemaking and tourism is that it is located at the most southern part of Canada—as far south as Northern California and farther south than over one-half of the United States. The Island's climate is unique and sustains rare forms of flora and wildlife.

The Island has a rich heritage. One can see the ruins of the first commercial winery built in Canada, Vin Villa. There are many ruins claimed by the Lake Erie. The Island is also well-known as the place where Al Capone smuggled rum into Ohio in the 1920's. There is an exhibit to mark the days of Prohibition.

The history is in the wine.

Peninsula Ridge Estates Winery Winemaker: Jean-Pierre Colas

www.peninsularidge.com

I was over come with awe when I first saw the magnificent Victorian home located on the winery property. I felt like I was in another time and another place.

Visually reminiscent of some wineries found in the Napa Valley, this winery was officially opened in 2000. Winemaker, Jean-Pierre Colas is well versed in making great wine. His 1996, Chablis Grand Cru, Les Clos, was chosen, 'White Wine of the Year' by *Wine Spetator Magazine* in 1998.

Sporting a modern underground barrel cellar, historic restaurant, and a spacious retail shop, Peninusla Ridge produces great and powerful wines. A must taste for any connoisseur is the red, Arcanum (a Meritage blend with added Syrah) and the white, Chardonnay INOX.

Pillitteri Estates Winery Winemaker: Sue-Ann Staff

www.pillitteri.com

When Gary Pillitteri was an amateur winemaker, he won a gold medal for his Icewine. Some years later, in 1993, he started his own winery. His son and daughter, Charles and Connie, also contribute to the family business.

Recently, a new underground barrel cellar was completed and the winery and boutique are being renovated.

Winemaker, Sue-Ann Staff's credo is to produce the finest wines possible from the highest quality Niagara Peninsula grapes. Sue-Ann has a B.Sc., Agriculture (University of Guelph) and a Graduate Degree, Oenology (University of Adelaide, Australia).

It is true that Pillitteri produces some truly 'avante garde' wines, the Merlot and Cabernets are truly amazing in both concentration and power. Nevertheless, it seems that the icewines are the most popular.

By far, Pillitteri is the biggest icewine producer in Canada. They offer a variety of wines such as Vidal, Chardonnay, Riesling, Cabernet Sauvignon, Cabernet Franc and, of course, the sparkling Icewines.

Reif Estates Winery Winemakers: Klaus Reif and Robert DiDomenico
www.reifwinery.com

When Klaus Reif was a boy, he used to play hide-and-seek in the huge wine fermentation barrels at his family's winemaking facility in Germany's Rhine Valley. His descendants have been making wine since the sixteenth century. Following in the family tradition, Klaus went on to earn degrees in Oenology and Viticulture from Geisenhiem University. He opened his doors to Reif Niagara in 1983.

Robert DiDomenico (Sp. Honours, Microbiology, Univeristy of Guelph) joined Reif in 1990. Together with Klaus, they have steadily worked to develop and improve an already great product.

Reif Estates wines are powerful and elegant—qualities that is hard to beat. "Nature makes wine," Klaus says. "We make great wine by producing premium grapes." So it stands, from his first growth of Ultra Premium Reds to his dessert wines, Reif Estate wines reflect the best that nature has to offer.

Southbrook Farms Winemaker: Colin Campbell
www.southbrook.com

Bill Redelmeir, owner of Southbrook, started this boutique winery in 1991. Present winemaker, Colin Campbell joined on in 1995. Together, Southbrook has won over 150 international medals and trophies. In 2005, its wines and fruit wines came won four medals at the Ontario Wine Awards and seven medals at the All Canadian Wine Awards.

Southbrook's wines have proven age ability. Even its base wine, Southbrook Red, comprised of Marechal Foch, can age for at least 4 years while the premium Southbrook Triomphe has a recommended span of 15 years. The whites are just as amazing with an average span of three years and 11 years of age potential for the Triomphe Chardonnay.

The dessert wines are all exceptional; culminating in an absolutely magnificent Framboise d'Or, made with very rare golden raspberries grown in St. Catherines.

Southbrook began as (and still is) one of Ontario's largest roadside markets and pick-your-own produce farms. The farm eventually expanded to making great wines.

Stratus Winemaker: J-L. Groux
www.stratuswines.com

In 2000, Daivd Feldberg purchased 25 hectares and succeeded to hire winemaker, J-L. Groux. Stratus officially opened in June 2005. J-L Groux, was born and raised in the Loire Valley, France. He studied winemaking in Burgundy and he continues to hone is skills at the University of Bordeaux. He immigrated to Canada in the early 1980's and joined Hillebrand Estates in 1989. He is now the winemaker at Stratus, which is owned by David Feldberg.

J-L insists on low yield grapes that are strictly controlled in every facet. His Stratus Red and White contain blends of several vinifera grape varieties. They are ultra-premium wines that have already captured the interest of experts. J-L also has another wine that is called 'Wild Ass', which is comprised of wines that do not make the Stratus standard. This 'art of assemblage' allows Mr. Groux to achieve his goal of 'finesse, longevity and integration'.

Stratus has already gained notoriety as being the first winery to achieve the LEED Certificate granted by the Canada Green Building Council. LEED standing for 'Leadership in Energy and Environmental Design'. The certificate is awarded to businesses that are constructed and operate with minimal impact on the environment. Some of the features include geothermal technology to heat and cool the building, recycled material used in construction and design, organic landscaping, toxin-free waste management program and energy efficient systems.

Ever since he joined the Canadian wine scene, Mr. Groux has been regarded as a 'Traditional Innovator'. His place in Canadian wine history has certainly been affirmed.

Stoney Ridge Winery Winemaker: Lubimir Popovici
www.stoneyridge.com

The story of Stoney Ridge has as many levels as the bouquet of a fine wine. The winery began in 1985 when Jim Warren founded Stoney Ridge. The winery was very successful, however, Jim retired from Stoney Ridge in 1999 to work as a consultant at Niagara College's Teaching Winery. Jim did return to Stoney Ridge to work with Chief Winemaker Lubimir Popovici. Together they created the Founder's Signature Collection. Popovici has won several outstanding awards for his own wines and continues to use his innovative ways to develop further outstanding wines. The future looks bright for Stoney Ridge Winery.

The Grange of Prince Edward County Winemaker: Jeff Innes
www.thegrangewines.com

The focal point of this winery is an 1830 barn built by United Empire Loyalists. It has been carefully restored over time. The 50 or so acres of well-drained clay gravel soil provides for over 50,000 vines (all vinifera). Burgundian methods of viticulture are practiced, including hand harvesting of both red and white grapes. The red vinification involves long maceration periods of 15 to 30 days, punching down of Caps twice per day and aging in French oak barrels. The whites are gently de-stemmed, crushed and fermented slowly at cool temperatures. The Chardonnay is aged from 6 to 8 months in French oak barrels.

The winery produces Pinot Noir, Chardonnay, Cabernet Franc, Pinot Gris, Gamay and Riesling.

Manitoba Wineries

D D. Leobard Winery Winemakers: Dennis d'Eschambault and Leonard Streilein
www.ddleobardwinery.com

The first D.D. Leobard wines were released to the public in 2000. Their dry strawberry wine was an immediate success. By 2001 the company's sales were up 170% and by 2003 they were producing a host of fruit wines ranging from Black Raspberry on Strawberry to Wild Blueberry. That year the Iced Strawberry, Wild Blueberry Dessert Wine and Wild Blueberry Wine won Bronze medallions at the Canadian Wine Awards. The medals grew to two Silver medals in 2004 and a Silver medal at the All Canada Wine Championships in 2005.

Not wanting to limit their great success at home, the winery is marketing their wines in South East Asia, China, Europe and the United States.

One of their many exciting creations is a truly unique wine made from the Birch tree. Aptly called 'Birch Wine', it is described as 'taken from the Birch tree deep in the Northern Canadian boreal forest. This wine is comparable to any fine white wine. I was curious to find out more about this distinctive wine. Denis explained, 'If you can imagine, it has been compared to a Chardonnay with a Sauvignon Blanc or Pinot Gris or Riesling blend. It is earthy or woody depending on who is making the comments. As we ferment it out completely, the wine still has a slight sweet finish. I have poached fish in it and have had wonderful comments. Any reduction will sweeten it and bring out wonderful flavours as well. We have to keep in mind that this raw material is reduced to make syrup at a ratio of 100:1. Goes great with oysters, shrimp and shellfish. We are just now able to give it to some chefs to 'play' with, and we are looking forward to some great recipes.' So are we!

Alberta Wineries

Fieldstone Fruit Wines Winemaker: Dominic Rivard
www.fieldstonefruit.com

In 2005, Fieldstone Fruit Wines became Alberta's first cottage winery. On 50 acres, this winery grows Bumbleberry orchards, which yields raspberries, black cherries, Saskatoon berries and strawberries. Their winemaker, Dominic, not only produces prized wines, he is also very active in promoting them all over the world—even China. Presently making high quality fruit and dessert wines, this winery is making a true name for itself.

British Colombia Wineries

Burrowing Owl Estate Winery Winemaker: Jim and Steve Wyse
www.bovwine.ca

Located in the very picturesque Southern Okanagan Valley, not far from Lake Osooyos, this winery officially opened in 1998, five years after owner, Jim Wyse, planted the vineyards. The vines are carefully cropped and the grapes are stringently selected.

The winery's philosophy is to co-existence with the natural environment. They take great care not to interfere with the dessert-like ecosystem. No artificial pest control is used and no animal, plant or mineral is harmed or misplaced in any way. In fact, their efforts are directed to saving the environment and the animals that share the winery. Captive breeding programs and 'Injured Bird of Prey' rehabilitation programs are strongly supported by the winery and its staff.

The winery boasts about having the first underground cellars in the Okanagan Valley. They produce some lovely wines, including 2002 Meritage, 2002 Merlot and 2002 Cabernet Sauvignon.

With state-of-the-art equipment and updates, this winery keeps moving forward.

Blasted Church Vineyards[90] Winemaker: Kelly Moss

www.blastedchurch.com

Owned by Chris and Evelyn Campbell, this winery is located in the small town of Okanagan Falls. The winery's name comes from a story that goes back to 1929, when a 103 year old church was moved from a small deserted mining town to Okanagan Falls. Apparently, dynamite was used to dismantle the church. The name, Blasted Church Vineyards, was chosen to honour its history. In fact, you will find a little bit of history (and humour) behind every delicious bottle of wine—with telling names such as Hatfield's Fuse, That Dam Flood, Blasphemy, and so on.

Winemaker Kelly Moss established an unbeatable reputation as an assistant winemaker at Calona Vineyards before joining Blasted Church. The winery has won top awards for its wines. You will enjoy their Unoaked Chardonnay Musque, (Gold, Canadian Wine Championships), Pinot Gris (Gold, CWC) and Rose (Gold, CWC). The winery also holds a superb Gospel Midnight Service with great music and food. Check the website for details.

Hawthorne Mountain Vineyards Winemaker: Dave Carson

www.hmvineyard.com

Hawthorne Mountain Vineyards is situated on one of the highest points in the Okanagan. From there, one can see Lake Skaha and the valley below.

Hybrid vines were initially planted in the early 1960's, but over time they have been replaced with vinifera plantings of Merlot, Pinot Noir, Chardonnay, Pinot Gris, Ehrenfelser, Riesling and Gewurztraminer. The cool climate allows for the fresh flavour of these grapes to come through.

The wines are indeed impressive. The Pinot Noir has excellent length and wonderful fruit—a perfect expression of the terroir.[91] In 2003, Hawthorne Mountain released a new wine series, "See Ya Later Ranch" wines, to give recognition to the site's 'quirky' history and Major Hugh Fraser (1885-1970) who was the first to grow grapes on the property. He would be proud to know that Hawthorne Mountain Vineyards is VQA member.

Lotusland Winery Winemaker: David Avery
www.averyfinewine.ca

Located in the Fraser Valley near Abbotsford, Lotusland was called A'Very Fine Winery but changed the name to the present one in 2003. David and Liz Avery began planting in the late 1990's. Their vineyard is scrupulously organic and their wines are exceptional. Lotusland is well known for their superb vinifera reds (Pinot and Merlot) as well as their whites (Chardonnay, Pinot Gris, Gewurztraminer and Rainbow Blend). A popular feature at the winery is a monthly cooking class instructed by a well-known local Chef.

The winery is planning on building another winery and a golf course. A'Very Fine Wine is now a brand name for wines under the major Lotusland Brand (http://www.lotuslandvineyards.com/).

Mission Hill Winery Winemaker: John Simes
www.missionhillwinery.com

Located in the central Okanagan valley, Mission Hill was originally founded in 1966, but the story actually begins much later (about 1981) when Anthony von Mandl bought and completely revamped the winery—hiring the best architects and builders to produce a spectacular winery. In 1996, he began growing his own vineyards, which now number to a select five: Osoyoos Vineyard Estate, Oliver Vineyard Estate, Naramata Ranch, Pinehill Vineyard Estate and Mission Hill Road Vineyard Estate. Each has its own unique microclimate suited to specific varieties of Mission Hill Vines.

Winemaker, John Simes is very proud of the job the Mission Hill team does in making wine. A native of New Zealand, Simes wasn't new to winemaking when he joined Mission Hill in 1992. His reputation was already established when he made wine for Montana Wines, one of New Zealand' most prestigious wineries. John received the coveted International Wine and Spirits Competition (IWSC) award twice in five years.

Mission Hill wines reflect their talent and dedication. They produce a variety of wines from the five vineyards. The Oculus is the Estates signature wine.

Nk'Mip Cellars Winemaker: Randy Picton
www.nkmipcellars.com

In August 2002, Nk'Mip Cellars Winery (pronounced inkameep) opened its doors. A joint venture between the Osoyoos Indian Band and Vincor International, Nk'Mip uses grapes that are harvested solely from the Band's own Inkameep vineyard.

Situated on the beach overlooking the shores of Osoyoos Lake, the view from the winery is stunningly beautiful. The winery is adjacent to a tract of natural desert land.

While wine is the main trust of this enterprise, visitors can find out about the Band's history and traditions. The architecture of the winery is designed to complement the native art and artifacts as well as enhance the desert surroundings.

The winery uses modern equipment such as grape crushers, pumps and presses specially selected to gently handle the grapes, juice and wine.

Winemaker, Randy Picton (Business Administration, Mount Royal College, Calgary; Winery Assistant Program, Okanagan University College, Penticton) was trained by Jackson-Triggs and B.C. winemaker, Bruce Nicholson. Presently making several wines, Chardonnay, Merlot, Pinot Noir, Pinot Blanc, the winery has won numerous medals including gold for its magnificent icewine.

Orofino Vineyard and Winery Winemaker: John Weber
www.orofinovineyards.com

Nestled in Crawston, a town within the Similkameen Valley, this new winery is constructed using technology that has been around for over 200 years. The Orofino Winery is Canada's only winery built out of environmentally friendly, straw bales.

Recently, the winery won a gold medal for their Merlot/Cabernet blend. Critics are also raving about Orofino's great Pinot Noir. The winery also produces a Late Harvest Muscat and a Pinot Gris. This winery is off to a flying start.

Osoyoos-Larose Winemaker: Pascal Madevon

Website not yet available

Osoyoos-Larose is a collaborative effort between Vincor and Bordeaux giant, Group Taillan.[92] It is ideally located on the southernmost part of the

Okanagan Valley, just north of the U.S. border, where it enjoys low rainfall, excellent drainage and a great deal of sunlight. Under such conditions, the vines develop exceptionally well and disease is kept to a minimum. Even Don Triggs, President and CEO of Vincor International, was surprised by success of the first vintage in 2001. "We didn't expect this quality from 3 year old vines." When winemaker Pascal Madevon, first arrived from Bordeaux and tasted the grapes, he decided "my new country [is] Canada!" Mr. Merlaut (Director General of Group Taillan) sums it best: "We started with a piece of land that we did not know what was possible to do. We thought it was a great location for making great wines. However, we never realized that the ecosystem of this unique wine-growing area would have such a dramatic effect on the speed that our young vines would develop and on the quality of their fruit."

No expense was spared in the developing of this magnificent winery. World famous wine consultant Michael Roland and wine expert Alain Sutre oversaw the development of the vineyard and winemaking. Sutre even designed and custom built the winery's fermentation tanks.

The initial vintage was made with 66% Merlot, 25% Cabernet Sauvignon and 9% Cabernet Franc. The blend has a multitude of taste levels such as raspberry, spice, and pepper and vanilla on the nose with a palate flavour of chocolate, raspberry and anise.

The winery is planning on adding two more wines to their list: Petite Verdot and Malbec.

Sonoran Estate Winery Winemaker: Arjan/Ada Smits

www.sonoranestate.com

Sonoran Estate Winery has a breathtaking, panoramic view of Lake Okanagan, the vineyards and orchards of Naramata, and the wild splendour of Okanagan Mountain Park. Planted with Pinot Blanc, Gewurztraminer, Merlot and Pinot Noir, this estate allows one to totally explore the senses. Here, you can relax and enjoying as much as you want. The B&B[93] located on the property will make you want to stay.

Sumac Ridge Winery Winemaker: Mark Wendenburg

www.sumacridge.com

Sumac Ridge was founded in 1980 by Harry McWatters. Involved with the B.C. wine and restaurant industry since 1968, Mr. McWatters was named to the

B.C. Restaurant Hall of Fame (January 17, 2005). His contributions towards the making of quality wine and introducing the V.Q.A. to B.C. are legendary.

British Colombia's oldest estate winery is also one of its most decorated. Its wines, which are made from 100% B.C. grapes, won 22 medals in the 2004 Okanagan Fall Festival Judging Awards.

Township 7 Winemaker: Cory Coleman and Bradley Cooper
www.township7.com

In 1999, Corey and Gwen Coleman bought five acres of land in Langley B.C. to plant a vineyard. Their winery opened in 2001. In 2004, after acquiring seven acres, they established another winery and tasting boutique on the Naramata Bench in the Okanagan Valley.

Cory and Gwen focus on the production of small lots of high quality Merlots, Cabernets, Syrahs, Chardonnays, Pinot Noirs, Sauvignon Blanc and Semillon grapes. They take great pride in the outstanding quality they produce. They also use grapes selected from the fruitful and abundant vineyards in the Oliver area of B.C.

Their wines received honours at the Canadian Wine Awards, the B.C. Wine and Oyster Festival and the prestigious, 2nd Annual Lieutenant Governor's Awards of Excellence in British Colombia Wines. Even England's top wine guru, Jancis Robinson, gave top marks to three of their wines: Township 7 Chardonnay Reserve 2002, Merlot 2001, and Syrah 2002.

Cory and Gwen's wines are causing quite a stir. With only a few years under their belt, their future holds much promise.

Quebec Wineries

Vignoble le Cep d'Argent Winemakers: Jean-Paul and Francois Scieur
www.cepdargent.com

Vignoble le Cep d'Argent is located in the Eastern Township of Quebec Province. Owned by Denis Drouin, it is the Townships' most northerly winery, not far from Sherbrooke, and just across the Chemin de la Riviere highway from beautiful Petite Lac (Lake) Magog. In 1985, some 10,000 Seyval Blanc vines were planted. The varieties now planted include Seyval, Guysenheim, Cayuga, Marechal Foch, De Chaunac, and Ste. Croix.

Winemakers Jean-Paul and Francois Scieur are sixth generation winemakers. They are the first to make Sparkling Wine in Quebec—which is little wonder, seeing that the brothers are from Champagne. The winery produces lovely wine that promises to get even better. Vive La Provence!

Prince Edward Island Wineries

Rossignol Estate Winery Winemaker: John Rossignol
www.rossignolwinery.com

In 1990, John Rossignol moved to Little Sands, Prince Edward Island[94] where he started to make his own wine. It is Prince Edward Island's only winery—and what a winery!

Mr. Rossignol's innovation resulted in unique grape and fruit blends that won two silver medals in 1997 at the prestigious Intervin Wine Competition for his Seyval Blanc and Marechal Foch wines. More recently, Rossignol wines won three gold medals for their Rossignol Blackberry Mead, Rossignol Maple Wine and Isle Saint-Jean and two silver medals, at the All Canada Wine Awards in 2005. The Isle Saint-Jean is one of John's new wines—a great blend of Blueberry and Marechal Foch that many critics say is reminiscent of fine Bordeaux.

John's initiative and imagination led him to 'house' more tender vinifera grapes such as Cabernet Franc, Merlot and Chardonnay in greenhouses[95] and reputed to be the only winemaker/viticulturist that uses greenhouse grapes in Canada—possibly anywhere!

At Rossignol Estate, the belief is that the traditional wines of the Maritimes are indeed fruit wines. Fruit wines made from strawberry, apples, raspberry, blue berry and rhubarb comprise much of the estate's 45,000 bottles of wines. Their grape varieties include Marechal Foch, Seyval Blanc, Valiant, Pinot Noir, Cabernet Franc and Chardonnay.

The labels on their bottles are works of art. They are yet another expression of the talented hands of winemaker and winery builder, John Rossignol.

Nova Scotia Wineries

Blomidon Ridge Estate Winery Winemaker: Wes Lowrey
www.blomidonwine.com

Known as 'Canada's Tidal Winery', this estate, located near the town of Canning along the shores of the Bay of Fundy's Minas Basin, is affected by the movement of the tides. "The changes of air over the vineyard twice per day keep the grapes dry and relatively disease free," says Wes Lowery, Vineyard Manager and Winemaker.

The land used to be owned by Habitant Vineyards, but it is now the property of the McCains, which also has holdings in Ontario's Niagara Bench region.

Vineyards include Chardonnay, Baco Noir, L'Acadie Blanc, New York Muscat and Seyval Blanc.

Gaspereau Vineyards Winemaker: David Gardner

www.nswine.ca

The grand Gaspereau Valley surrounds the vineyard and winery. The Red Barn style boutique, which encompasses store and winery, is impossible to miss as one descends the valley. They produced red wines such as DeChaunac, Lucie Kuhlmann, Port (m/d) and white wine, including L'Acadie Blanc, Muscat Dry, Ortega Vidal Icewine and Maple Wine. All of their wines are medal winners.

Domaine de Grand Pré Winemaker: Jurg Stutz

www.grandprewines.ns.ca

Having bought the winery in 1993, Hanspeter Stutz wanted to develop distinctive Nova Scotia wines from techniques, methods and grape varieties specifically designed for Nova Scotia. A passionate man, he deserves the recognition that he is getting.

The winery is a showpiece with a grand view of the Bay. You can enjoy a meal either outside on the patio or in their fabulous restaurant, Le Caveau.

Daughter Beatrice handles the hospitality. Her husband, Alex Jurt, is the Chef. Hanspeter's son, Jurg is the winemaker. Jurg was educated in viticulture, winemaking and marketing at Waedenswill, Switzerland. He oversees production on the 15-acre vineyard and acreage in the Gaspereau. Grand Pré's distinctive wines have won medals in such events as the Canadian Wine Awards, All Canadian Wine Championships, Finger Lakes International Wine Competition and InterVin International. One of their new additions is the 100% Nova Scotian Sparkling Wine made with Vidal Blanc as a base and three flavours: Maple, Peach and Blueberry. Hanspeter Stutz has a great deal to be proud of!

Jost Vineyards Winemaker: Hans Christian Jost
www.jostwine.com

Geisenheim-trained winemaker, Hans Christian Jost, took over the reins of the family business when his father, German winemaker (and Rhine winery owner), Hans Wilhelm Jost, passed away in the late 1980's.

The original vineyard was planted in 1978. Presently, the 45 acres of vineyards can be found in Malagash, along the Northumberland Strait, just off the Sunrise Coast. And they have vineyards in the Gaspereau Valley further south.

The winery obtained its license in 1983 and officially opened its doors in 1985. The wines are produced from a variety of grapes: Marechal Foch, L'Acadie Blanc, Muscat, Leon Millot, Geisenheim, Seyval, Vidal, Michurinetz,[96] Severnyji[97] as well as Chardonnay, Zweigelt and Cabernet Sauvignon and Cabernet Franc.

To ensure supply and quality, Jost Vineyards has over 130 acres under contract with grape growers throughout Nova Scotia and also imports vinifera grapes (Chardonnay) from Ontario.

Jost has won many medals in world competition including a 'Canada Wine of the Year' in 2000 for its 1999 Vidal Icewine. His Marechal Foch Reserve, Baco Noir Reserve (Double Gold Winner) and Muscat Icewine (Double Gold Winner) are superb.

Newfoundland Wineries

Weil Winery[98] Winemakers: Winston Jennings and Edward Weiterman
www.weilwinery.com

Weil Winery was started in 1998 on the island of Twillingate[99] in Newfoundland. The wines are made from the finest fruits and berries and only purified water is used to make the wine. The whole winemaking process and bottling is done on the premises. This allows for strict quality control of all steps during the winemaking. Weil makes wines for every meal and occasion. They come in beautifully designed bottles with a picture of sailing vessels (called Bankers) on their labels. Bankers were a fleet of ships used to receive freshly caught cod in order to salt them.

People commonly do not know that Newfoundland produces wines, let alone excellent wines; however, Weil has certainly proved them wrong. After all, Newfoundland has been in the winemaking business a long time.

New Brunswick Wineries

Winegarden Estate Ltd.

www.winegardenestate.com

Trail Blazers come in many forms. In New Brunswick, a province not normally associated with wine, Winegarden Estate has a reputation for innovation and technological advancement. They produce first-rate wine by accommodating the climate of New Brunswick, selecting grape varieties that can flourish within its parameters, and relying on their skills as wine connoisseurs and vintners.

The family has long been in the winemaking business. In 1860 the great grandfather of the Werner Rosswog family, Johann Ziegler, received the right to distill fruit from the Grand Duke of Baden, Germany. Generation after generation, the family made excellent fruit distillates. In 1983 they immigrated to Canada where they carry on the fine tradition. In 1999, Elke and Stefen Rosswog joined the family business.

Premium wines, brandy, Schnapps, and liqueurs are among the 50 or so products they sell—all made from homegrown fruit. In 2004, the first New Brunswick 'L'Acadie Blanc' grape was introduced. Somehow, I think that this is only the beginning of the many innovations that Winegarden Estates will introduce.

Ferme Bourgeois Farms

www.fermebourgeoisfarms.ca

Belliveau Orchards and Bourgeois Farms are nestled in the Memramcock Valley in New Brunswick, just outside Moncton (Pré-d'en-Haut). The orchards began in 1932 and were later purchased by Cleric, Father Azarias Massé in 1955. La Maison Ste. Croix, located next to the orchards, was built by Father Massé. He entrusted the operation of the orchards to the same family that manages it today.

The property is the sight of many events during the harvest season. People from all over the world visit the estate to taste the many styles and types of fruit wines they make, including apple, pear and cherry as well as icewine, still/flat wine, sparkling wine and cider.

CANADA'S WINERIES 'SEA TO SHINING SEA'

Wineries listed in *italics* are featured in the chapter describing the wineries and are paired with the recipes.

Newfoundland

There is some argument as to where Leif Ericson landed when he called the land 'Vineland'. Romantics want to believe that it was Newfoundland at Lance aux Meadows.

While Newfoundland is not ideally suited to growing grape vines, especially vinifera grapes, great wine is made here from berries and fruit.

Rodriques Markland Cottage Winery	(709) 759-3003
Weil Winery	(709) 884-2707

Nova Scotia

Nova Scotia has truly focused its winemaking talents to the specific grapes, climate and soil of the region. Nova Scotia's proximity to large bodies of water (Bay of Fundy, Northumberland Strait, Atlantic Ocean) allow grapes (some vinifera and French Hybrids) to grow healthy and abundant, especially in the Annapolis and Gaspereau Valleys and the North Shore (Malagash). They produce superb wines ranging from age-able reds, fragrant whites and succulent dessert wines.

Andres Wines	(902) 461-8173
Bear River Winery[100]	(902) 467-4156
Benjamin Bridge[101]	
Blomidon Estate Winery/Habitant	(902) 582-7565[102]
Cabot Wineries	(902) 420-9463
Grand Pre Vineyards	(902) 542-1753
Gaspereau Vineyards	(902) 542-1455[103]
Jost Vineyards	(902) 257-2248 1-800-565-4567
Petite River Winery	(902) 688-2295
Sainte Famille Wines	(902) 798-8311

	1-800-565-0993
L'Acadie Vineyards	(902) 542-3034[104]
Lunenberg Country Winery	(902) 644-2415
Williamsdale Winery	(902) 686-3117
	1-800-439-1224

Prince Edward Island

P.E.I. has only one winery, but I've added it to my list of favourite places to tour. French Hybrids flourish and vinifera do thrive under the 'glass' of a greenhouse. Again, the maritime climate supports an abundance of healthy vines.

Rossignol Estate Winery	(902) 962-4193

New Brunswick

New Brunswick's climate is conducive to fruit farming. In some microclimates, grape wines are produced. The Memramcook Valley and the microclimate just off the Northumberland Stait are some of the sheltered areas where fruit and grape wine are made.

Belleisle Vineyards	(506) 485-8846
Belliveau Orchard	(506) 758-2325
Gagetown Cider Company	(506) 488-2147
Ferme Bourgeois Farms	(506) 758-02956
La Ferme Maury	(506) 743-5347[105]
Tierney Point Winery	(506) 755-6492
Tuddenham Wines	(506) 466-1840
Winegarden Estate Ltd.	(506) 538-7405

Quebec

Quebec's harsh climate seems a very unlikely spot for Canadian winemaking, but wine has been a staple in this province since the very beginning of settlement in the 15th and 16th centuries. The wineries are basically small, family-owned and operated businesses. 'Hilling' or 'shoring' is generally used to protect the vines from the extreme temperatures and drying winds of winter.

Clos St. Denis	(450) 787-3766
Domaine Felibre[106]	(819) 876-7900
Vignoble de la Sabliere	(450) 248-2634
Domaine Royarnois	(418) 827-4465
Vignoble Domaine de l'Adennais	(450) 248-0597
Domaine des Cotes d'Ardoise	(450) 295-2309[107]
Vignoble de l'Orpailleur	(514) 295-2763
Vignoble la Bauge	(514) 266-2149[108]
Vignoble le Cep d'Argent	(819) 864-4441
	1-877-864-4441
Vignoble les Blancs Coteaux	(450) 295-3503
Vignoble les Pervenches	(450) 293-8311
Vignobles des Negondos	(450) 437-9621[109]
La Roche des Brises	(450) 472-2772
Riviere du Chene	(450) 491-3997
Vignoble de Lavoie-Poitevin	(450) 469-3894
Vignoble Clos De La Montagne	(450) 358-4868
Vignoble Trois Clochers	(450) 295-2034
Vignoble des Pin	(450) 347-1073
Vignoble Cappabianca	(405) 691-1515
Vignoble Angell	(450) 246-4219
	Montreal - (450) 522-1012
Vignoble Morou	(450) 245-7569
Vignoble Le Royer St-Pierre	(450) 245-0208
Vignoble du Marathonien	(514) 826-0522
	(514) 321-9347
Vignoble Mission du Vigneron	(450) 263-1524
Domaine du Ridge	(450) 248-3987
Clos Ste-Croix de Dunham	(450) 295-3281
Artisans du Terroir	(450) 379-5353
Vignoble Sainte-Petronille	(418) 828-9554
Isle de Baccus	(418) 828-9562
Carone Vineyard[110]	(514) 240-4220
	(514) 630-4146
Domaine Royarnois[111]	(418) 827-4465
Vignoble le Moulin du Petit Pre[112]	(418) 824-4411

Ontario

Ontario is looked upon as the standard by which Canadian wineries measure their wines. Ontario's microclimates are conducive to growing superb grapes and making fine wine.

The Niagara Escarpment is made up of some 7 different climatic zones. Lake Erie North Shore and Pelee Island have excellent microclimates with ample sun, temperature, rainfall, drainage and soil structure. Add technology and winemaking skills and you get one of the grandest wine producing regions of the world.

Niagara Peninsula

Andres Wines	(905) 643-8687 1-800-836-3535
Angels Gate Winery	(905) 563-3942
Birchwood Estate	(905) 562-8463
Chateau des Charmes	(905) 473-2273
Caroline Cellars	(905) 468-8814
Cave Spring Cellars	(905) 562-3581
Creekside Winery	(905) 562-5493[113]
Crown Bench Estates	(905) 563-3959
Coyote's Run	(905) 682-8310 1-877-269-6833
De Sousa Wine Cellars	(905) 563-7269
Domaine Vagners	(905) 468-7296
EastDell Estates	(905) 563-5463[114]
Featherstone Estate Winery	(905) 562-1949
Fielding Estate Winery	(905) 563-0668 1-888-778-7758
Flatrock Cellars	(905) 562-8994
Frogpond Farm	(905) 468-1079
Henry of Pelham Family Estate Winery	(905) 684-8423
Herender Estate Wines	(905) 684-3300
Hidden Bench Vineyards	(905) 563-8700
Harbour Estates Winery	(905) 562-6279 1-877-439-9163
Harvest Estate Wines	(905) 682-0080

Hillebrand Winery	(905) 468-7123[115]
Inniskillin	(905) 468-2187 1-888-466-4754
Jackson-Triggs Niagara	(905) 468-4637 1-888-702-8527
Joseph's Estate	(905) 468-1259 1-866-468-1259
Kacaba Vineyards	(905) 562-5625
King's Court Winery	(905) 687-8965
Kittling Ridge	(905) 945-9225
Konzelmann Estate Winery	(905) 935-2866
Danial Lenko Wines	(905) 563-7756
Laily Vineyard	(905) 468-0503
Lakeview Cellars	(562) 562-5685
Le Clos Jordan	(905) 562-9409
Legends Estate Winery	(905) 563-6500
Magnotta Winery	(905) 563-5313 1-800-461-9493
Maleta Winery	(905) 685-8486[116]
Malivoire Wine Company	(905) 563-9253
Maple Grove Winery	(905) 562-7415[117]
Marynissen Estates	(905) 468-5784
Mountain Road Wine Company	(905) 563-0745
Niagara College Winery	(905) 641-2252
Palatine Hills Winery	(905) 646-9517
Peller Estate Winery	(905) 468-4678
Peninsula Ridge Estates Winery	(905) 563-0090
Pillitteri Estates Winery	(905) 468-3147
Puddicombe Estate Farms and Winery	(905) 643-1015
Reif Estate Winery	(905) 468-5878
Ridgepoint Wines	(905) 562-8853
Riverview Estate Winery	(905) 262-0636
Rockway Glenn Estate Winery	(905) 641-1600 1-877-762-5929
Royal DeMaria Winery	(905) 562-6767
Stonechurch Vineyards	(905) 935-3535
Stoney Ridge Estate Winery	(905) 562-1324

Stratus Wines	(905) 468-1806
Strewn Estate Winery	(905) 468-1229
SunnyBrook Farm Estate Winery	(905) 468-1122
Tawse Winery	(905) 562-9500
Thirteenth Street Wine Co.	(905) 562-5900
Thirty Bench Winery	(905) 563-1698
Thomas & Vaughan	(905) 563-7737[118]
Trillium Estate Winery	(905) 684-4419
Vineland Estate Winery	(905) 562-7088 1-888-846-3526
Willow Heights Winery	(905) 562-4945

Lake Erie North Shore[119]

This region enjoys a similar climate as the Niagara Peninsula. The Escarpment provides greater protection from harsh climate conditions than the Blenheim-Ridgetown Gravel Ridge, but the moderating effect of Lake Erie has a comparable, positive impact on the grapevines.

Colchester Ridge Estate Winery	(519) 738-9800
Collio Estates Winery	(519) 738-2241 1-800-265-1322
D'Angelo Estate Winery	(519) 736-7959
Eric Shore Vineyard and Winery	(519) 738-9858[120]
Grape Tree Estate Wines	(519) 322-2081
Leblanc Estate Winery	(519) 738-9228
Sanson Estate Winery	(519) 726-9609
Viewpointe Winery	(519) 738-4718 (519) 738-2421

Pelee Island

This island enjoys the moderating effect of Lake Erie, plus it has more heating units[121] than any other spot in Canada—a historic wine area with unmatched beauty and points of interest.

Pelee Island Winery	(519) 733-6551 1-800-597-3533

Prince Edward County

One of the newer regions, Prince Edward County has good growing season but winters can be harsh—very harsh. The number of wineries is increasing fueled by a number of celebrities and wine critics.

Black Prince	(613) 476-4888
	1-866-470-9463
County Cider Company Estate Winery	(613) 476-1022
Carmela Estates Winery	(613) 399-3939
	1-866-578-3445
Della-Gatto Bella Vineyards	(613) 476-4888[122]
By Chadsey's Cairns Winery	(613) 399-2992
Long dog Vineyard and Winery	(613) 476-4140
The Grange of Prince Edward Estate	(613) 399-1048
	1-866-792-7712
Prince Edward County Wine Growers Association	(613) 471-1006
Peddleston Wines Ltd.	(613) 399-3939
Huff Estates Winery	(613) 393-5802
Waupoos EstatesWinery	(613) 476-8338
Closson Chase Vineyards	(613) 399-1418
Norman Hardie Wines	(416) 407-9752
Fieldstone Estate Vineyards	(613) 399-1176[123]
SugarBush Vineyards	(613) 849-0521
33 Vines	(613) 373-1133

Eastern Ontario

Le Domaine Cervin	(613) 448-2245

Western Ontario

Western Ontario is not known for its wine. The region is usually lumped together with Lake Erie North Shore. However, there are enough wineries to warrant a place of their own.

Bellamere Country Market and Winery	(519) 473-2273
George Smith Vineyards	(519) 676-5867
Birtch Farms and Estate Winery	(519) 469-3040
Brus Orchards and Winery	(519) 842-2262
Carolinian Winery	(519) 268-2000
Rush Creek Wines	(519) 773-5432
Cox Creek Cellars	(519) 767-3253
Downey's Estate Winery	(905) 838-2990
Meadow Lane Winery	(519) 633-1933
Munro Honey & Meadery	(519) 847-5333
Norfolk Estate Winery[124]	(519) 586-2237

Greater Toronto Area

The GTA is a very large 'catch-basin' of wineries that do not fit in any other area or region. Many of the wineries use both innovative and traditional ways to produce award-winning wines.

Applewood FarmWinery	(905) 642-4720
Archibald Orchards and Estate Winery	(905) 263-2396
Cilento Wines	(416) 264-9463
Magnotta Winery	(416) 735-7551
	1-800-461-9463
Milan Wineries	(416) 740-2005
Muskoka Lakes Winery	(405) 762-3203
Nesher Wines	(416) 631-6727
Ocala Orchards Farm Winery	(905) 985-9924
Scotch Block Country Winery	(905) 878-5807
SouthBrook Farms Winery	(905) 832-2548
Whittamore's Farm Winery	(905) 294-3275
Willow Springs Winery	(905) 642-9463

Manitoba

Manitoba's climate is quite extreme with temperatures ranging as high as 30° C to as low as -30° C. Nevertheless, award winning fruit wines are produced here.

D.D. Leobard Winery (204) 661-9007[125]
Rigby Orchards Ltd. (204) 523-8879[126]

Saskatchewan

Even with a continental climate tougher than Manitoba, Saskatchewan still has still managed produce two fruit wineries!

Aspen Grove Winery (306) 771-2921
Banach Winery (306) 445-9463

Alberta

Warm summers and frigid winters are the rule. Alberta's first cottage winery opened its doors in July 2005. They make outstanding fruit wines.

Fieldstone Fruit Wines (403) 934-2749

British Colombia

British Colombia comes close to challenging Ontario for quality wine. B.C. has the right climate and soil to produce first class wines. The province has proven its ability time after time at national and world compctition.

Much of the glory goes to the Okanagan Valley Wine Region, but other regions such as Similkameen, Vancouver Island Regions and Fraser Valley are also productive with new wineries springing up every year.

Fraser Valley

Fraser Valley is home to the Fraser River in the southwest part of British Colombia. Its moderate climate has drawn a mixture of fruit and grape wineries.

Lotus Land Winery (604) 857-4188[127]
Domaine de Chaberton (604) 530-1736[128]
1-888-332-9463

The Fort Wine Company	(604) 857-1101
	1-866-921-9463
Glenugie Winery Ltd.	(604) 539-9463
	1-866-233-9463
Township 7 Vineyards and Winery	(604) 532-1766
(Okanagan Location of Township 7)	(250) 770-1743
Well Brook Winery	(604) 946-1868

Vancouver Island

The Vancouver Island region produces some excellent wines. Vancouver Island boasts the mildest climate in Canada. Summertime is warm and sunny, with frequent ocean winds. Temperatures reach average highs in the mid-20's C, but evenings can be cool. The Vancouver Island region is the most temperate of all British Columbia, with temperatures just below 0° C during winter. This can allow for good grape development—especially whites. The other islands are somewhat drier. Red grapes for both the Fraser and Vancouver/Gulf area sometimes imported from the warmer Okanagan Valley. Many fruit wines also made.

Alderlea Vineyards Ltd.	(250) 746-7122
Averill Creek	
Blue Grouse Estate Winery	(250) 743-3834
Chalet Estate Winery	(250) 656-2552
Chateau Wolff	(250) 753-4613
Cherry Point Vineyards	(250) 743-1272[129]
	1-866-395-5252
D'Asolo Vineyards	(604) 871-4329
Garry Oaks Winery	(250) 653-4687
Glenterra Vineyards	(250) 743-2330
Honeymoon Bay Winery	(250) 749-4681
Malahat Estate Winery	(250) 474-5129
Marshwood Estate	(250) 285-2068
Middle Mountain Mead Winery	(250) 336-1392
Morning Bay Vineyard	(250) 629-8361
Saturna Island Vineyards	(250) 539-5139[130]
	1-866-918-3388
Salt Springs Vineyards/Longharbour	(250) 653-9463

Venturi-Schultze Vineyards	(250) 743-5630
Victoria Estate Winery	(250) 252-2671
Vigneti Zanatta Winery	(250) 748-2338
Echo Valley Vineyards	(250) 748-1477 or 1470 (store)
Godfrey-Brownell Vineyards	(250) 748-4889 or 715-0504
Marley Farm Winery Ltd.	(250) 652-8667
Merridale Estate Cidery	(250) 743-4293
Thetis Island Vineyards	(250) 246-2258
Township 7	(604) 532-1766[131]
Tugwell Creek Meadery[132]	(250) 642-1956
Westham Island Estate	(604) 940-9755
Winchester Cellars	(250) 544-8217
Church and State Wines[133]	

The Okanagan/Similkameen Valleys

The Okanagan Valley is unbelievably beautiful. The scenery is as diverse as the wines and wineries, which range from small, family-owned vineyards to huge estates with magnificently built mansions. The Okanagan can be divided geographically into North and South regions (although there are many microclimates in between). The northern half is colder and receives substantially more rain than the southern side.

The smaller Similkameen Valley is west of the Okanagan. The climate is much like southern Okanagan[134] with very dry, desert conditions.

The following wineries are listed in alphabetical order for all areas in the Okanagan and Similkameen Valleys.

Adora Estate Winery	(250) 404-4200 1-866-404-9463
Arrowleaf Cellars	(250) 766-2992
Bonaparte Bend Winery	(250) 457-6667[135]
Bella Vista Vineyards	(250) 558-0770
Benchland Vinyards Winery	(250) 770-1733 1-800-610-3794[136]
Blackhills Estate Winery	(250) 498-0666
Blasted Church Vineyards	(250) 497-1125

Blue Montain Vineyard	(250) 497-8244
Burrowing Owl Vineyards	(250) 498-0620
	1-877-498-0620
Calliope Vineyards	(250) 494-7213
	1-866-366-0100
Calowna Wines	(250) 762-9144
	1-888-246-4472
Carriage House Wines	(250) 498-8818
CedarCreek Estate Winery	(250) 764-8866
Crowsnest Vineyards	(250) 499-5129
Columbia Gardens Vineyard and Winery	(250) 367-7493[137]
D'Angelo Vineyards	(250) 493-1364
	1-866-329-6421
Dirty Laundry Vineyards	(250) 494-8815[138]
Dessert Hills Estate Winery	(250) 498-1040
Domaine Combret	(250) 498-6966
	1-866-Terroir
Elephant Island Orchard Wines	(250) 496-5522
Fairview Cellars	(250) 498-2211
First Estate Cellars	(250) 767-9528
Foxtrot Vineyards[139]	(250) 767-9528
Gersighel Wineberg	(250) 495-3319
Gehringer Brothers Estate Winery	(250) 498-3537
	1-800-784-6304
Golden Mile Cellars Estate Winery	(250) 498-8330
Granite Creek Estates Wines	(250) 835-0049
Gray Monk Cellars	(250) 766-3188
	1-800-663-4205
Hainle Vineyards Estate Winery	(250) 767-2525
Harmony-one Vineyards	(250) 499-2144
Hawthorne Mountain	(250) 497-8267
HerderWinery and Vineyards	(250) 499-5595
Hester Creek Winery	(250) 498-4435
Hillside Estate Winery	(250) 493-6274
	1-888-923-9463
House of Rose	(250) 765-0802
Hunting Hawk Vineyards	(250) 546-2164

Inniskillin, Okanagan	(250) 498-6663
	1-800-498-6211
Jackson-Triggs Okanagan	(250) 498-4981
Joie Wines	1-866-422-5643
Kettle Valley Farm Winery	(250) 496-5898
La Frenz Winery	(250) 492-6690
Lang Vineryards	(250) 496-5987
Larch Hills Winery	(250) 832-0155
Laughing Stock Vineyards	(250) 493-9463
Little Straw Vineyards Winery	(250) 769-0404
Mission Hill Family Estate Winery	(250) 768-7611
Mistral Estate Winery	(250) 770-1733[140]
Mount Boucherie Estate Winery	(250) 769-8803
	1-877-684-2748
Nichol Vineyard	(250) 496-5962
Orofino Vineyards and Winery	(250) 499-0068
Osoyoos-Larose	(250) 498-4981[141]
Paradise Ranch Wine Corp	(604) 683-6040[142]
Pemberton Valley Vineyards	(604) 894-5857
Pentage Winery	(250) 493-4008
Pinot Reach Cellars	(250) 764-0078
	1-877-764-0078
Popular Grove Winery	(250) 492-4575
Quails Gate Estate Winery	(250) 769-4451
	1-800-420-9463
Raven Ridge Cidery	(250) 763-1091
Recline Ridge Vineyards and Winery	(250) 835-2212
Red Rooster Winery	(250) 492-2424
St. Laszlo Vineyards	(250) 499-2856
St. Hubertus Estate Winery	(250) 764-7888
	1-800-989-9463
Sandhill Wines	(604) 267-9463
	1-888-246-4472
Sonoran Estate Winery	(250) 494-9323
Scherzinger Vineyards Cottage Winery	(250) 494-8815
See Ya Later Ranch	(250) 497-8267
	1-800-998-2255[143]

Silver Sage Winery	(250) 498-0310
Spiller Estates Winery and B&B	(250) 490-4162
	1-800-610-3794[144]
Stag's Hollow Winery	(250) 497-6162
	1-877-746-5569
Sumac Ridge	(250) 494-0451
Summerhill Pyramid Winery	(250) 764-8000
	1-800-667-3538
Thornhaven Estates Winery	(250) 494-7778
Tinhorn Creek Vineyards	(250) 498-3228
	1-888-484-6467
Township 7	(250) 770-1743
Van Western Winery[145]	
Wild Goose Vineyards	(250) 497-8919

A PLACE TO GO–A PLACE TO STAY[146]

Touring wineries is great fun. However, at the end of the day, you won't want to hurry home in rush hour traffic. Nothing beats a great meal, nice surroundings, comfy sofa, hot shower, and cozy bed! The countryside has many places to stay—most very good and some great! Here are some places that you may wish to consider while traveling through Canada's wine regions.

There are, of course, many superb Bed and Breakfasts throughout Canada. The ones that I describe are unique. I highly recommend that you stay at one of these establishments during your next cross-country tour. For further listings and information, visit *Bed and Breakfast Online_Canada* (www.bbcanada.com).

Newfoundland

Kelsie's Inn

www.kelsiesinn.com
24 Toulinquet Street, P.O. Box 784, Twillingate, Newfoundland A0G 4M0
(709) 884-1290, 1-888-884-1290

The island and town of Twillingate is located on the shores of Notre Dame Bay. The area was named by French fishermen who compared it to the 'Toulinquet' isles off the coast of France. The island was an important seaport and trade centre in the 1600's and 1700's. Although the French fished for cod in the area, it was the English who eventually settled on the island.

Kelsie's Inn is rated 3.5 stars by Canada Select. The inn recently expanded by adding six double rooms (16 in total) and a large sitting room. All accommodations have private bathrooms with showers. Continental breakfast is included. It is a very pleasant inn with high standards.

Situated on an island steeped in history and places to see, Twillingate and Kelsie's Inn are definitely for me.

Crewe's Heritage Bed & Breakfast

http://www.angelfire.com/nf/crewe/bb.html
33 Main Street, Twillingate, Newfoundland
1-866-884-2723

Not far from Weil Winery is a historic Bed & Breakfast that was built in the early 1900's by Captain John Butcher. This is truly an amazing place where one can view icebergs and whales on one side of the harbour and pick wild berries on the other. You can take a leisurely hike along a near by hill to get an excellent view of the harbour and see spectacular sunsets.

Crewe's Heritage has three rooms, all with private baths, and a great deal of homemade bread, jams and muffins. Mmm!

Prince Edward Island

Bayberry Cliff Inn

www.bayberrycliffinn.com
Route # 4, Little Sands, Prince Edward Island, C0A 1W0
1-800-668-3395

Overlooking the warm waters of the Northumberland Strait, just minutes away from the Wood Islands Ferry Terminal, is the very elegant Bayberry Cliff Inn. Located in Little Sands, this Bed & Breakfast offers four spacious living accommodations ensconced in Maritime beauty.

Rooms are fitted with large windows and private decks where you can see seals and porpoises, bird and other animal life. For those interested in getting some exercise and adventure, you can follow the Confederation Trail and walk along seemingly endless beaches, coves and places of historical interest.

Several fine restaurants are situated within 30 minutes of Prince Edward Island's only winery, Rossignol Estates, which features unique blends and viticultural methods.

Enjoy your privacy. Commune with nature. Experience the history. Sip the wine. Love the food. Visit the Bayberry Inn!

My Father's House Bed and Breakfast

www.myfathershouse.ca
1262 Route 18, Murray Harbour, Prince Edward Island, C0A 1V0
1-877-292-3655

Just 20 minutes from the Wood Island Ferry, this Bed & Breakfast is a Canada Select 4 Star establishment. It has three rooms: one with two double beds, and an en suite full bathroom with a complete kitchen and washer and dryer. The other two rooms have en suite full baths and queen beds. All rooms have cable television, private phone, and a river view. And, the 7th day of your stay is free!

Imagine waking up to birds singing and hearing the wild call of gulls while they circle above the South River. It is a peaceful fishing village of about 350 people.

Here you can take in the various activities such as jogging, cycling, seal and bird watching, beach combing, clam hunting and shopping for crafts during the day. At night you can visit the area theatre or relax on the deck of the screened verandah, sipping wine created only 20 minutes away at the Rossignol Winery. Life doesn't get much better than this.

Nova Scotia

The Train Station Inn

www.trainstation.ns.ca
21 Station Street, Tatamagouche, Nova Scotia, B0K 1V0
902-657-3222, 1-888-724-5233

Imagine spending a night in a train station or a railway caboose. *The Train Station Inn* is spacious, full of character, elegant, comfortable and very, very romantic.

This one hundred year-old station has been restored to provide travelers with a very unique lodging experience. The main station (former stationmaster's residence) has three bedrooms, private baths, a parlor, sitting rooms, balcony, and kitchenette. The main floor has a museum, café and gift shop.

The cabooses range from 27 to 94 years of age, but they are remarkably preserved. Each lodging includes a queen-sized bed, fireplace, air conditioning, television, private bath and railway memorabilia.

The Tatamagouche station was built in 1887 and officially closed in 1973, although rail service stopped a year prior. It was slated for demolition but was purchased by owner James Lefresne (at that time just 18 years old and full of idealism). Restoration started in 1987 (100 years after the station was built) and has been on going.

Continental breakfast is included with your stay. Located on Sunset Trail, it is an ideal place for sight seeing, and there are golf courses and art galleries only minutes from one of Nova Scotia's best vineyards—Jost!

Victoria's Historic Inn & Carriage House

www.victoriashistoricinn.com
600 Main Street, Wolfville, Nova Scotia
1-800-556-5744

Victoria's Historic Inn & Carriage House is a five star Registered Heritage Property built in 1893 by William Henry Chase.

Not far from Grand Pre Vineyards, in the picture postcard town of Wolfville (the home of Acadia University), this stunningly beautiful home is currently owned by Sherrie, Steven, and their parents Urbain and Carol Cryan.

Samantha, the black house cat will surely be on hand to greet you as you arrive, along with hostess extraordinaire, Claire Davidson, who is always on hand to assist in any way.

The Inn has nine luxurious rooms, each equipped with a television, VCR, CD player, bathrobes, hairdryer and air conditioner. The honeymoon suites offer fireplaces and double Jacuzzis. Each room comes with a private four-piece bathroom. The rooms are decorated with many antiques. The Carriage house, which was built some time later, has seven rooms with private entrances. All the rooms are exceptionally designed and are unique in their comfort and attractiveness. Breakfast is included in the price and does not leave you wanting. The coffee flows freely. If you're lucky, Thomson, the other household cat whose purr can be heard from across the room, will visit your table.

There is plenty of sightseeing around beautiful and scenic Wolfville. Wine lovers can travel to the lovely Grand Pre Vineyards, Gaspereau Vineyards and Benjamin Bridge Vineyards,[147] as well as visit Blomidon (formerly Habitant) and Sainte Famille Wineries, which are a must see for any oenophile.

The Victoria's Inn and Carriage House certainly lives up to its five star rating.

New Brunswick

Indian Point B&B Motel[148]

www.new-brunswick.net

323 Fort Rd. P.O. Box 1555, Port Elgin, N.B. E4M 3Y9

(506) 538-7586

One is greeted like home in this eleven unit B&B, which is located right next to a very scenic seashore and lighthouse at the mouth of the Gaspereau River and Green Bay. The comforts include satellite television, private bath, telephone, laundry facilities, canoe and bike rentals, propane barbecues and lawn chairs. The two bedroom condo-cottages (available with kitchenette, microwave, dishes, utensils, linen and towels) are absolutely beautiful. Breakfast is available.

Local attractions include beaches, ecological parks, rock formations, national parks and golf courses—all within easy reach of this B&B. There is, of course, Winegarden Estates in Baie Verte where one can sample the good wines of New Brunswick. A place to visit—and stay awhile!

Les Trois Moulins

www.bbcanada.com/6168.html

172 route La Vallee, Memramcook, New Brunswick E4K 2A6

(506) 758-0911, (506) 850-1266

Les Trois Moulins has four rooms: three with shared bath and one with private bath. Full breakfast is provided. This is one of my favourite places to relax.

The region has a rich heritage. Here you can learn about Acadian culture and enjoy the splendour of Memramcook Valley.

I recommend visiting La Ferme Bourgeois Winery and Belliveau Orchards or take advantage of special packages that include golfing, bird watching, sporting events and nature retreats.

Quebec

Auberge L'Etoile-sur-le-Lac

www.etoile-sur-le-lac.com

1200 Principale Street, West, Magog, Quebec J1X 2B8

(819) 843-6521, 1-800-567-2727

Just one hour out of Montreal and a few minutes from the great Cep d'Argent Winery is a luxurious inn and condominium development that sparks romanticism in the heart and adventure in the soul. Here you can sip wine while taking in the panoramic view that stretches down the lake to the Green Mountains of Vermont. This European style complex offers closeness to a 2.5 kilometre (about 1.5 miles) long shoreline park on the shores of Lake Memphremagog. It is close to shops in downtown Magog, ski resorts, and golf courses as well as great wineries.

The Auberge L'Etoile-sur-le-Lac has 53 rooms including 27 deluxe rooms and 2 suites. All the deluxe rooms and suites come equipped with queen bed, sofa bed, armchairs, television, phone, worktable and computer connection as well as therapeutic bath and hairdryer. Most have fireplaces and overlook the lake.

For those who fancy great food, the L'Ancrage restaurant and courtyard café features Mediterranean style food as well as a patio bistro. For those who love sports and leisure, they offer lounging at the outdoor heated pool, sailing, water skiing, cruises and walking paths.

Ontario

Niagara Peninsula

Vintage Inns
www.vintageinns.com
1-888-669-5566 or

The Prince of Wales Hotel and Spa; Queens Landing Inn and Conference Centre; and The Pillar and Post Inn, Spa and Conference Centre joined together in 1997 to become a favourite destination for travelers the world over.

The Prince of Wales Hotel and Spa
6 Picton Street, Niagara-on-the-Lake, Ontario L0S 1J0
905-468-3246

Those who think that they are being royally treated at this hotel are correct. The hotel is named after George, Prince of Wales (later King George V), who stayed there in 1901.

The hotel, with its 112 rooms, has all the modern comforts, but reflects an age of elegance and refinement. The rooms are individually decorated in a Victorian design with the finest of furnishings.

They also have a Secret Garden Spa for sensual pampering, and a magnificent restaurant for fine dining. If you are feeling less formal, you will enjoy the pleasant menu at the Churchill Lounge or the Tapas Wine Bar.

The Hotel and Spa is in the midst of Niagara-on-the-Lake where you can venture out for a stroll after dinner or try a buggy ride or browse the various shops. There are numerous parks within walking distance and, of course, Lake Ontario and Niagara River are close by.

Queen's Landing
155 Byron Street, Niagara-on-the-Lake, Ontario L0S 1J0
905-468-2195

The grand Georgian manor, with its lavish entrance, gives the appearance of the 'deep south' rather than southern Ontario. I imagine hearing Rhett Buttler's words, "Frankly Scarlett…!'

This elegant manor has 144 rooms, over half of which are equipped with either a whirlpool and fireplace or some rooms have both features. There are dining areas at Queen's Landing—the Tiara Restaurant offers a panoramic view of the historic Niagara-on-the-Lake Harbour as well as fine original cuisine created from organic ingredients grown on local farms. For a more causal atmosphere, try the Bacchus Lounge or the ultra relaxing barbecue on the Landing's patio.[149]

The Inn has an indoor pool and spa plus special services for banquets, conferences and business needs.

Only a short walk to Niagara-on-the-Lake, Queen's Landing is synonymous with the finest in pleasure and a must for any rendezvous.

The Pillar and Post Inn, Spa and Conference Centre
48 John Street, Niagara-on-the-Lake, Ontario L0S 1J0
(905) 468-2123

What started out as an 1890's canning factory is now a 123-room five star[150] country inn where the services verge on decadence and cuisine will please any palate. The Pillar and Post Inn is known far beyond our shores.

The original bricks and beam construction reflects the building's colourful past. The fine furniture, skylights, terracotta tiles and ever-present flowers bring the colourful past into the bright present and glowing future.

A wide range of activities are available. You can swim in the heated salt water pool, swirl around in a turbulent whirlpool, or melt away under a gentle, soul fulfilling massage.

The Pillar and Post has it all: wine country, great cuisine and relaxation, and it is within reach of the heart of Niagara-on-the-Lake.

Grand Victorian
www.grandvictorian.ca
15618 Niagara Parkway, Niagara-on-the-Lake, Ontario L0S 1J0
905-468-0997

Formerly called 'Riverscourt', the history of this house dates back to around 1870 (1801, if you include the former house that was on this property). The oak Chippendale staircase descends from the top floor to the great hall. The stained glass windows are pierced with multi, laser like, pencils of sunlight, touching parts of the original oak ceiling high above the main floor. The spectacular, Grand

Victorian, with its 12 foot ceilings, is located in Niagara-on-the-Lake next door to world famous Reif Estates Winery and it is not far from Inniskillin wines.

This building has a rich heritage. It was owned by counts, businessmen, politicians and wealthy Americans, all of whom added their personalities to it. Signatures of builders from 1884 are etched within the house's dumbwaiter.

There are six large elegant guest rooms furnished with antiques and four-poster beds. One can keep warm by the fireplace in winter and cool down on the porch during a warm summer night. A walk through the garden or by the river in the morning before a brunch style breakfast is a great way to start the new day. Solace, peace and meditation can be yours or you can attend the many events at Niagara-on-the-Lake and wine country.

Grand Victorian—history in the making.

Inn on the Twenty

www.innonthetwenty.com
3845 Main Street, Jordan, Ontario L0R 1S0
(905) 562-5336, 1-800-701-8074

Located at Cave Spring Cellars Winery in the Village of Jordan, this unique inn was the vision of Leonard Pennechetti. Originally a century old warehouse (which had an underground connection to the winery), it was renovated into a luxurious and decadently comfortable inn, with all the comforts. Stones from a torn down century old building in New York were used to build the Inn on the Twenty and On the Twenty Restaurant.

The rooms and various areas around the inn are decorated with various original works of art, antiques and contemporary furniture. Every room is unique, and each will please.

Next to the inn is Vintage House, a former Bed and Breakfast built in 1840, which is now part of Inn on the Twenty. It once served to accommodate seasonal workers for the old Jordan Winery (parts of which can be still be seen in the barrel cellars of Cave Springs). It features three suites decorated in the original colonial style.

There are many points of interest just outside Inn on the Twenty. Besides the award-winning cuisine of On the Twenty Restaurant and decorated wines of Cave Spring Cellars, there are a myriad of antique, art and heritage shops, including a lovely and unique garden centre.

There are a number of get-away packages for the adventurer or you can just ease yourself into the inn's reputable spa.

Whether its excitement you want or just a quiet vacation, Inn on the Twenty has it all.

Gatehouse Hotel

www.gatehouse-niagara.com

142 Queen Street, Niagara-on-the-Lake, Ontario L0S 1J0

905-468-3263

Gatehouse Hotel has been described as the best-kept secret in the Niagara Peninsula. Located at the west end of Niagara-on-the-Lake, this superb mansion has retained its character despite the modern style of its outstanding restaurant, Ristorante Giardino. The Italian deco and clean lines of the architecture lend an open elegance to the dining area. The food and service is four stars and the price is very reasonable.

The Gatehouse Hotel is a short five-minute walk from most of the interesting destinations of Niagara-on-the-Lake. Several wineries are only a few minutes away.

Lake Erie North Shore

Kingswood Inn

www.kingswoodinn.com

115 Mill Street West, Kingsville, Ontario N9Y 1W4

(519) 733-3248

The Kingswood Inn was built by Col. James S. King in 1859. Located in Kingsville,[151] the inn is situated on three acres in the southernmost part of Canada. It has a two-story guest apartment that features a full kitchen, dining room, living room, television/vcr and private entrance. Suitable for any length of stay, it offers an in ground pool, continental breakfast, coffee maker, dishes and many other amenities.

Apart from enjoying a walk through the inn's beautifully landscaped garden, one can appreciate the closeness to Lake Erie North Shores' and Pelee Island Wineries and other attractions such as bird watching tours, national parks, Zen gardens, antique shops, fine dining and casinos.

A magnificent spot for the wine lover and adventure seeker!

Telegraph House Bed and Breakfast
www.telegraphhouse.com
205 Main Street, Port Stanley, Ontario, N5L 1C4
(519) 782-3006

This historic Bed and Breakfast is built on the foundations of another historic home. Postmaster Manuel Payne built this house in 1875 on the original foundations of what was called the Bostwick House.[152] Payne ran the post office next door and also brought the telegraph system to Port Stanley, which served as an early warning device for ships on Lake Erie.

After a few incarnations some years later, Chefs, Jon and Vicci Coughlin bought and renovated the building to its present form. They designed and decorated three beautiful rooms, each with large en suite bathroom. The house has two working fireplaces and wireless Internet. Breakfast is served either on the porch or main dining room. You must try the yellow perch and eggs in season. The dining room is open to the public for lunch all year round.

With much to see and do (including some great local wineries), this place is a must for the traveler.

Pelee Island

Twin Oaks Retreat, Bed & Breakfast
www.peleeisland.net
Pelee Island, Ontario N0R 1M0
(519) 724-2434, 1-877-735-3366

Located on beautiful Pelee Island, Twin Oaks' very spacious farmhouse and sprawling property is ideal for groups and families. The grounds are home to rare flora such as the Chinquapin Oaks, Prickly Pear Cactus, Sassafras, Honey Locust and Hop Tree.

Guests sit on the verandah and relax while watching the plethora of colourful bird. Others find shade under the exotic trees to catch up on the latest books.

Pelee Island has a lot to offer You can swim, walk or hike or ride a bicycle. If you're really looking for adventure, you can go diving to see historical nineteenth-century ship wrecks.[153] You can also tour the historical light houses,[154] nature reserves,[155] and wildlife areas[156] or simply go fishing.[157]

A major tourist destination is Pelee Island Winery.[158] Two of the exhibits located at the winery are the winery tour features an antique European grape press and a demonstration on how corks are made. Visitors can also participate in a wine tasting. Incidentally, Bed & Breakfasts on Pelee Island stock Pelee Island wine, which is perfect for the occasion.

There is more happening on the Island than I can mention.[159]

Prince Edward County

Miller's House—Bed & Breakfast

www3.sympatico.ca/millerhouse
2843 County Road 10, Milford, Ontario K0K 2P0
(613) 476-6715

This early nineteenth-century house was built by James Clapp. His father built the first two mills in the Milford area circa 1800-1810. James built several mills in the area including Scott's Mill, which can be seen from the Miller's House—B&B. This picturesque house is on the banks of Black Creek and overlooks a waterfall and pond as well as a spacious, well-landscaped, garden lot.

There are four spacious bedrooms plus a dining room and living room. Two of these rooms have their own en suite with sitting area while the others have shared en suites. A full breakfast is provided and for earlier risers there is coffee and orange juice. Bicycle tours and picnic lunches can be arranged. Of course, there are other wineries of Prince Edward County that beckon as well as Sandbanks Provincial Park.

Covent Garden Bed and Breakfast

www.coventgarden.ca
303 Main Street, Wellington, Ontario K0K 3L0
(613) 399-2981, 1-888-505-7773

Escape to Prince Edward County and lose yourself at Covent Garden B&B. This is not a huge establishment (it consists of two glorious rooms each with its own private bathroom or en suite), but the Victorian home decorated with art and antiques is one of your more interesting and intriguing ones.

Covent Garden is located close to all that is interesting and beautiful in Prince Edward County—its wineries (of course), golf clubs, Provincial Parks

(Sandbanks), gourmet shops, museums, horseback riding, fishing, shopping and absolutely wonderful people. The most attractive feature, however, is the Covent Garden Fine Art Gallery, which is located next to the B&B.

Owners Michael Deyell and Dean Munro are Toronto advertisers known as the 'Welly Boys'. They have been commissioned by some heavy weight companies such as Harlequin Enterprises, Heart and Stroke Foundation, Mitsubishi Motors, Corel, National Art Gallery, Toronto Dominion Bank and Sandbanks Project. They are currently promoting Canadian and American Artists. They represent over 25 Canadian and American artists. Mediums include oil, watercolour, acrylic, fibre, glass, wood, metal, clay and ceramic.

They formed a group of artists called 'Q7'. The seven artists in this group reside in the Bay of Quinte area and are promoted by Michael and Dean throughout Canada and the United States.

Devonshire Inn on the Lake

http://www.devonshire-inn.com
24 Wharf Street, Wellington, Ontario K0K 310
(613) 399-1960, 1-800-544-9937

Wake up to a view of Lake Ontario, birds flying in the distance or stroll through the garden during summer when the humming birds flitter in and out by the flowers and kingfishers fish in the creek. Sit and listen to the waves and enjoy the scene.

The inn was originally built as a foundry in the 1870's and was converted to private residences in the 1890's. Now, the Devonshirc is an intimate country resort nestled on the waterfront of Prince Edward County.

The seven rooms (one is actually a suite of 2 rooms) are spectacular and impeccably decorated, each unique, and each with their own grand view. The food is fantastic and the atmosphere decadently cozy.

Imagine it in winter—cozy, beautiful, a roaring fireplace, bottle of wine, and two glasses.

Durham Region

Hillcrest Inn Bed and Breakfast
www.hillcrestbedandbreakfast.com
2996 Concession Rd. 8, RR# 5, Bowmanville, Ontario
(905) 263-9988, 1-866-771-2184

Hillcrest Inn Bed and Breakfast is just a 'hop, skip and a jump' away from world famous speedway, Mosport. Hillcrest features four deluxe spacious rooms, each with air conditioning, private entrance, en suite bathroom, fridge/stove/coffeemaker, sitting area, and breakfast is provided in the morning.

The Tyrone Mill is a local historical attraction you can visit; and don't forget to try their pies! Hillcrest is near to Archibald Orchards and Estates Winery and 30 minutes away from Ocala Orchards Farm Winery, just north of Whitby.

The owners, Tony and Trallee Fanara, are very hospitable—they aim to please. This is an ideal spot for exploration, adventure and romance.

Willow Pond Country Bed and Breakfast
2640 Concession 7, Tyrone (Bowmanville), Ontario
(905) 263- 2405, 1-866-261-7494

There are many relaxing activities that await you at Willow Pond Country Bed & Breakfast. You can walk through ten landscaped acres on the fifty-acre farm, stroll alongside a wooded creek, watch the large goldfish feeding in the pond, swim in a heated pool, and fish for salmon in Lake Ontario or go snowmobiling in winter.

The inn is close to Archibald Orchards and Estates Winery, where they have delicious wines, great food and interesting curio items as that can be purchased as mementos or gifts. Just down the road from the winery are the 170-year-old Tyrone Mill and Ocala Orchards Farm Winery.

The inn has spacious rooms (with air conditioning and private en suites), luxurious surroundings and great hosts.

There are many more activities that you can enjoy at this lovely resort, including a superb Christmas Luncheon.

Lakeshore Bed and Breakfast
435 Lakeshore Drive, Port Perry, ON, L9L 1N7
www.bbcanada.com/lakshorebb
(905) 985-7684

Carolyn and Gerald West have a pleasant and very scenic Bed & Breakfast overlooking beautiful gardens and Lake Scugog. There are three exceptional rooms all with private bathrooms or en suites. Breakfast is served either in the dining room or the balcony overlooking the lake.

The residence is just minutes away from charming shops and restaurants, and only 20 minutes away from Ocala Orchards Farm Winery. Golf courses, lake-side walking trails, horseback riding, and a historic monument to the founder of Chiropractic are within easy reach.

Ezra Annes Bed and Breakfast
www.ezraannes.com
239 Wellington Street, Whitby, ON L1N 5L7
1-800-213-1257

This home was built over 200 years ago for Whitby's third mayor, Ezra Annes. His wife, Maria Losey, was the daughter of the area's first settler. The setting is charming and romantic; located on a quiet and picturesque part of Whitby, Durham Region's prosperous and scenic town. *Toronto Life Magazine* listed this B&B as 'A Perfect Getaway'—and so it is!

In 1992, this house was renovated to include en suite bathrooms and space for the collection of art and antiques. There are three ultra exquisite rooms with private en suite bathrooms.

Whitby is close to both Archibald and Ocala Wineries (about 30 minutes away). Guests can also visit the various points of interest such as Cullen Gardens and Miniature Village (closing January 2006), The Oshawa Parkwood Mansion, Auto Museum and the Whitby Heritage Homes.

This is a magnificent B&B. Try the gourmet Breakfast. A lovely place that is worth a five star rating!

Manitoba

Country Comfort B&B

www.bedandbreakfast.mb.ca/web2/index.shtml
Box 808, Killarney, Manitoba R0K 1G0
(204) 523-8742, 1-877-523-8511

This large ranch-style house has four comfortable rooms that can accommodate up to 16 people. The large farmyard, with its many trees, is an ideal spot for bird and animal watching, walking or just lazing around under the shade of an old tree.

Indoors, they have a large sunken entertainment area where you can easy back into one of their inviting chairs and watch a movie or read from their extensive library. Other recreational activities include cards, board games, shuffleboard and ping-pong tables. Golfing packages can be arranged and, of course, there is Rigby Orchards Winery, the beautiful gardens at the U.S.-Canadian Border, scenic swimming areas, wildlife museums, picnic areas and seasonal festivals.

Linda and Henry Krueger provide a full breakfast served on an antique table. Linda enjoys talking about cooking (she is a home economics teacher) and Henry raises purebred Angus cattle and is a cattle broker. Both love to travel and share stories with their guests.

Maison Grosvenor Bed and Breakfast

www.bbcanada.com/maison
824 Grosvenor Avenue, Winnipeg, Manitoba R3M 0N2
(204) 475-9630

This beautiful 1912 Queen Anne home has original stained glass windows, hardwood floors, oak staircase and ceiling beams.

Winnipeg's culture, cuisine and shopping can be experienced in one swoop. There is a myriad of shops in Osborne Village, Corydon Avenue houses Little Italy, and D.D. Leobard Winery is on DeBaets Street.

Maison Grosvenor B&B has three uniquely decorated guest rooms. Amenities include a kitchenette, telephone, Internet connection, television, outdoor hot tub, plus an easy going (and spotlessly clean) atmosphere. A healthy and varied breakfast is served in the formal dining room. Dietary restrictions can be accommodated.

They offer special theme packages such as 'Honey, It's Just You and Me'. If you get bored, 'Slick' the resident cat will discuss the day's events with you.

Saskatchewan

Creekside Terrace

www.creeksideterrace.sk.ca
2724 Angus Blvd., Regina, Saskatchewan S4T 2A7
(306) 569-2682

Welcome to a 1914 home that has solid oak woodwork, ceiling beams and a stone fireplace. Two rooms are available with private bath and television.

The building, which was constructed of materials originally intended for the Grand Trunk Hotel, is close to the Legislative Buildings. Creekside Terrace is centrally in the city of Regina and situated on the banks of Wascana Creek. The Devonian Trail is a great place for walking and biking.

You can take a tour of Aspen Grove Winery in White City or go dining, shopping and attending cultural events in Regina. Guest can also visit the historic town of Indian Head.

Antler Creek Bed and Breakfast

Box 302, Wawota, Saskatchewan S0G 5A0
(306) 739-2786
email: antlercreekb.b@sasktel.net

Helen and Lawrence Dezell's B&B has 7 bedrooms, 2 separate lounge areas and a private kitchen. They can accommodate large groups of 10 to 15 people or small family reunions. Tents can be pitched and evening campfires enjoyed.

Amidst beautiful parkland, cattle graze and the Dezells cut hay. For those of you escaping from the city, this 'touch of country' is truly what the doctor ordered.

Antler Creek is only 20 km east of Moose Mountain Provincial Park. At the park you join various outdoor activities and appreciate nature. Guest can also take advantage of local golf courses that will accommodate anyone from novice to pro. And, just minutes away, you will find historical sites, giant waterslides and gambling casinos.

On your way through southeast Saskatchewan, I recommend that you stop for a visit.

Alberta

Westways Bed & Breakfast

www.westways.ab.ca
216-25 Ave SW Calgary Alberta T2S 0L1
1-866-846-7038, (403) 229-1758

Westways Bed & Breakfast is about 45 minutes west from Strathmore—home of Fieldstone Fruit Wines. Hosts Jonathon Lloyd and Graham Mckay are proud of this 1912 Victorian Heritage home. They are one of the three licensed lodging houses in Calgary, which means that they are frequently inspected by the city. They maintain very high ratings with the Canada Select (4.5 stars), American Automobile Association (3 Diamonds) and Western Canada Bed and Breakfast Innkeepers Association.

The house is decorated with lavish with artwork, china displays, oil paintings, antiques and Persian carpets. Amenities include private bathrooms, tremendous food, voice mail, free movie channel and much, much more!

Westways is only minutes from an upscale area in downtown Calgary that has trendy restaurants, craft stores and parks.

The place is worth a visit. Here is what one guest had to say, "An ambience from days gone by and service with a smile. Spend some days at Westways—come tarry for awhile!"

Find all your yesterdays at Westways!

Rocking R Guest Ranch

www.rockingrguestranch.com
Box 45, Site 14, RR1, Strathmore, AlbertaT1P 1J6

Marvin and Terri Kinsman opened their new ranch on October 15, 2005. Guest can stay in a one or two bedroom cabins. Each cabin has a wood-burning stove and access to an outdoor fire pit and hot tub. The larger cabin has a full service kitchenette where your culinary imagination is only the limit. On the weekends they serve a wholesome and delicious two-course breakfast, while during the week, guests receive continental breakfast items, which they can enjoy at their leisure. The Kinsmans also offer spa and equestrian (horseback riding) packages.

There is much to see and do in this part of Alberta. Close by is the Fieldstone Fruit Winery, which opened in July 2005, and the historic Town of Strathmore, with its many seasonal events that range from the Christmas tree burning in January to the rodeos and heritage days in the spring and summer.

Any way you see it, this is a place to visit—you just might not want to leave!

British Colombia

Fraser Valley

Fenn Lodge Bed and Breakfast

www.fennlodge.com
15500 Morris Valley Road, Harrison Mills, British Colombia V0M 1L0
(604) 796-9798, 1-888-990-3399

Built in 1903, this property was restored in 1995. It has over 90 acres of landscaped and wooded ground. Visitors will enjoy the breathtaking scenery of the mountains, meadows, waterfalls and the Chehalis River. Nature is far and wide. The lodge has a variety of rooms; some have private bathrooms and others have shared facilities. Breakfast is provided and lunch and dinner can be arranged. Try it. Visit some wineries. Enjoy a romantic glass of wine at Fenn Lodge.

Traveller's Hotel Bed and Breakfast

www.travellershotel.ca
21628 48th Avenue, Langley, British Colombia V3A 3M8
905-604-533-5569

Sharon and Wally Martin restored this 1887 hotel back to its glory in 1999. The original building was built by Bill Murray to serve travelers heading for the Cariboo Gold fields. The Travellers Hotel is now considered a Heritage Site and has a five star rating for its five room accommodations and common areas. Each room has private shower and bath, individually controlled heating and cooling, and full breakfast (with special meals made under certain circumstances).

Here, the wine receives the atmosphere it deserves, and nearby you can visit Township 7, Lotusland and Gelnguie Wineries.

Okanagan Valley

Spiller Estates Winery and B&B

www.spillerestates.com
475 Upper Bench Road North, Penticton, British Colombia V2A 8T4
(250) 490-4162, 1-800-610-3794

What else could one ask for? A 1930's country home, the Okanagan Valley countryside, a winery with delicious fruit wines and a wealth of activities ranging from biking and swimming to golfing and or trying your luck at the casino.

There are four bedrooms available, each with an en suite bathroom or private bath. The country motif décor is complimented by the view of surrounding orchards, vineyards and the one-acre estate with its beautiful flowers, patios, pergolas and gardens.

Visitors can join in various activities or travel to Penticton's superb beaches.

You must take a tour of the Spiller Estate Winery, which features some of the world's best fruit wine made by Craig Larson. Craig also makes fabulous wines for Spiller's sister estates, Benchand Wines and Mistral Estate Winery.

To complement the fine service, a full breakfast is served with each nights stay. The Spiller Estates Winery and B&B are open from May 1st to the beginning of November.

Vineyard View Bed and Breakfast

www.dangelowinery.com
947 Lochore Road, Penticton, B.C. V2A 8V1
(250) 493-1364, 1-866-329-6421

Rise to the breathtaking view of Okanagan Lake and the surrounding mountains, which frame row upon row of vineyards. Imagine beautiful trails, beaches, hiking areas and wineries (Vineyard View is part of the D'Angelo Estate Winery).

This B&B has accommodations ranging from single rooms to a small private chalet. Each room has its own barbecue and private deck. The stay includes a self-serve breakfast, free local calls, parking, air conditioning, laundry facilities, swimming pool, and transportation to and from Penticton and Kelowna.

Windmill Bed and Breakfast

www.bbcanada.com/windmillbb

21606 Highway 97, Summerland, B.C. V0H 1Z6

You will find Windmill Bed and Breakfast at Sonoran Estate Winery. Here you can enjoy one of the fabulous four rooms that look over the Okanagan View while sipping Sonoran Pinot Noir or Merlot.

The B&B is a newly built new home with 1,200 feet of lakeshore. Amenities include a shared hot tub, pool, barbecue, kitchenette, television, library and Internet access. All rooms have private entrance, en suites, deck and fridge. There is a totally self-contained two-bedroom suite with private entrance and deck, although breakfast is not included with this room.

Full, continental, buffet, and vegetarian breakfasts are included with the rates for all other accommodations.

Windmill is close to Penticton's many recreational and shopping facilities.

FINAL NOTE: A REFLECTION

Wine can take you through an imaginative journey—a journey through time and space. When you open a bottle of wine, you're opening a time capsule that represents the land, culture, people, and knowledge of a past era.

I recently tasted an 1865 Chateau Villmaurine from St. Emilion, France (courtesy of Peter Mielzynski Agencies). The bottle came directly from the Chateau. In 1865, the American Civil War was coming to a close and President Abraham Lincoln was assassinated. Rudyard Kipling, author of *Jungle Book*, was born. The Salvation Army was founded and *Alice's Adventures in Wonderland* was published. Slavery was abolished and the Ku Klux Klan established. This wine was born when those events occurred over 140 years ago.

Imagine tasting a 1900 Haut Brion. Teddy Roosevelt was Vice President of the United States. William McKinley was President. Neither knew that McKinley would be felled by an insane man's bullet and Roosevelt would become President. Sir Wilfred Laurier was the Prime Minister of Canada. The Boer War was quite fresh in people's minds as was the invasion of Cuba and subsequent occupation by the Americans. World War I and the Titanic were not yet conceived. Cars were just being developed and flight—well, that was a just a dream. Russia and Japan had a conflict—which Japan somehow won. Mark Twain was still around and Albert Einstein was just getting started. Those who drink Molson's will appreciate that the Brewery was established around this time (1903). On a personal note, my grandmother celebrated her 10th birthday and my parents were not yet born.

Whenever I taste a vintage wine from any date, I experience my own personal time capsule. When I'm lucky enough to savour a 1945 Mouton, I taste the fruits of the year of my birth. (God, I'm old!) A 1950 reminds me of the year I immigrated to Canada. A 1978 captures the birth of my daughter Marisa and Taryn was born in 1993.

Many Canadian wines are age worthy because of the ingenuity of winemakers and the heartiness of vines to grow grapes under proper conditions over a consecutive number of years. These grapes will continue to flavour and fuel our wines to fulfill the legacy of the first plantings in Canada.

My trip across Canada has awakened my senses to the heritage of the wine. Whenever I sip Canadian vintage wine, I imagine historic events, the unfolding of time, and the creation of a grand nation—it has lived as we have lived. We see ourselves in the reflection of each bottle.

SUGGESTED READING

Denis D'Echambault, President of Manitoba's D.D. Leobard Winery, wrote, 'We can never have enough books on Canadian wines'. I believe that holds true for Canadian cooking.

For those who are interested in furthering their knowledge of wines from Canada and across the world, I have compiled a list of books for reference. I have also included some revered food and recipe books.

Wine Books

Adams, Leon D. 1990. *Wines of America*. McGraw-Hill.

Aspler, Tony. 1994. *Wine Lover's Companion*. McGraw-Hill Ryerson. Limited.

Aspler, Tony. Forthcoming 2006. *Wine Atlas of Canada*. Random House.

Aspler, Tony and Kathleen Sloan. 1999. *The Wine Lover Cooks*. Macmillan Canada. Aspler, Tony and Barbara Leslie. 2000. *Canadian Wine for Dummies*. John Wiley & Sons Canada Ltd.

Darling, Sheri. 2005. *Harmony on the Palate*. Whitecap Books.

Eberspaecher, Alex. 2002. *Vino Veritus*. Wine Cellar.

Hargrave, Lousia. 2004. *The Vineyard: A Memoir*. Penguin Group.

Johnston, Hugh. 2006. *Pocket Wine Book 2006*. Octopus Publishing Group Limited.

Schreiner, John. 2001. *Icewine: The Complete Story*. Warwick Publishing.

Schreiner, John. 2005. *Wines of Canada*. Mitchel Beazley.

Simon, Joanna. 1997. *Wine with Food*. Simon & Schuster Adult Publishing Group.

Ziraldo, Donald. 2000. *Anatomy of a Winery*. Key Porter Books.

Culinary Books

Armstrong, Julian. 2001. *A Taste of Quebec*. John Wiley & Sons.

Canadian Home Economics Association. 2001. *The Laura Secord Canadian Cook Book*. Whitecap Books.

Currie, Violet and Kay Spicer. 1993. *Full of Beans*. Mighton House.

Spicer, Kay. 1995. MultiCultural Cooking. Mighton House.

Kraft Kitchens. 2002. *Dinner on Hand*. Random House.

Lagasse, Emeril. 2005. *Emeril's Delmonico*. HarperCollins.

Lagasse, Emeril. 2004. *Emiril's Pot Luck: Comfort Food with a Kicked-Up Attitude.* HarperCollins.
Maximin, Jaqcues. 1986. *The Cuisine of Jacques Maximin.* Arbor House.
Montagne, Prosper. 2001. *Larousse Gastronomique.* Revised ed. Clarkson Potter.
Nightingale, Marie. 1989. *Out of Old Nova Scotia Kitchens.* Nimbus Publishing.
Oliver, Jamie. 2001. *The Naked Chef Takes Off.* H.B. Fenn & Company.
Stewart, Anita. 2000. *Flavours of Canada.* Raincoast Books.

Notes

[1] Vitis riparia is a wild species of grape variety that grows along stream banks, meadows and fences. It produces small grapes but can withstand a wide range of pests and climate extremes. Riparia is one of the vines used to develop new strains of 'quality' grapes that have some of the characteristics of vinifera species. Riparia rootstocks are also one of the species on which 'vinifera' cuttings are grafted.

[2] Phylloxera is a species of insect that feeds off the vine juices from the roots thus disenabling the plant from getting any nourishment to the leaves and thus killing the vine. Phylloxera was probably introduced to Europe by the importation of American plant cuttings and ended up devastating its vineyards. Grafting the vines to Phylloxera resistant American rootstocks was the major way that the European vineyards were saved.

[3] Grafting is a term used when a plant cutting is attached to another similar host plant in order to nourish and cultivate the cutting. This is done with apple trees and many other fruit species including grape vines.

[4] Labrusca is a species of North American grape vine.

[5] Hillebrand, was originally founded by Peter Mielzynski Sr. who also ran (and still runs) PMA, a very large Canadian Wine and Sprits importation company. Hillebrand is now part of the Andres Wine group.

[6] A vine or group of vines that is developed from the cuttings (asexual reproduction) of a vine that exhibits desired genetic characteristics. The differences may be very subtle but may be very important to the area. The inference here is that you can grow different types of vines from the same species i.e. Chardonnay or Pinot Noir. This is true to a point.

[7] This purchase was one of the reasons that led to Inniskillin's co-founder, Donald Ziraldo, to form the V.Q.A. or Vintners Quality Assurance.

[8] Up until Dr. Bannister broke that barrier, most runners thought he 'four minute mile' (now 1500 metres) was an impossibility. After Dr. Bannister's feat, it became an almost commonplace event.

[9] Pillitteri has added a cartouche (raise logo) featuring 'Pillitteri' on its bottles.

[10] A set of regulations governing all aspects of viticulture and viniculture.

[11] Statement of Goals and Purposes, Vintners Quality Alliance.

[12] See Chapter on Boutique wineries. Also check GATT and NAFTA.

[13] In 2001, the Jackson-Triggs state of the art winery in Niagara-on-the-Lake was opened with luxurious gardens and a superb, outdoor, amphitheatre, which hosts many of the world's greatest artists.

[14] At press time, the holdings are as follows: **CANADA:** Hawthorne Mountain Vineyards, B.C.; Inniskillin Okanagan; Inniskillin Wines, Niagara; Jackson-Triggs, Okanagan; Jackson-Triggs, Niagara; Sumac Ridge Estate Winery, Okanagan; Unity, Okanagan; Nk'Mip Cellars, Okanagan, Osoyoos-Larose, Okanagan **WORLD:** Goundrey Wines, Australia; Hogue Cellars, Washington; R.H. Phillips, California, Kim Crawford Wines, New Zealand; Kumala, South Africa.

[15] See also winery descriptions for Osoyoos-Larose, Jackson-Triggs Niagara, Delaine Vineyards, and Nk'Mip Cellars, Hawthorne Mountain and Sumac Ridge.

[16] The Wines of Ontario Sales and Marketing Plan: Poised for Greatness: A Strategic Framework for the Ontario Wine Industry, Wine Council of Ontario, 1999-2000.

[17] Niagara Peninsula and Lake Erie North Shore will be undergoing appellation changes over the next few years.

[18] Vintners Quality Alliance Ontario, 2004 Annual Report, Message from the Chair, page 3.

[19] Albeit many are fruit wineries compared to grape.

[20] 1 degree Brix equals 1 gram of sugar per 100 gram solution of grape must/juice.

[21] Although some excellent and luscious Non-V.Q.A. dessert wines are made (in similar style) from the New York Muscat grape in Nova Scotia.

[22] Introduced from Italy but, to my knowledge, is made in limited quantities at best.

[23] The author is glad the former option was chosen.

[24] An idea that is a pet project of Mr. Donald Ziraldo, whereby a whole tourist industry (i.e, lodging, hospitality, recreation Sites, festivals, etc.) has been developed with the vineyards as the centre or hub attraction.

[25] A bacterial (Leuconostoc Enos) fermentation, which, further 'mellows' the wine by fermenting left over sugar and malic acid into lactic acid thus adding complexity and richness to the wine.

[26] Champagne is a region just north east of Paris France. After much controversy, it has been ruled that only Champagne can call their wine Champagne.

[27] A measure of sugar water, i.e., cane sugar mixed with still champagne.

[28] If you are left handed, reverse this process using right hand to hold cork and left hand to twist.

[29] Aroma is usually referred to as the natural characteristic smell of the grape variety in the wine, especially when the wine is young.

[30] Bouquet refers to the complex interaction that occurs after fermentation, aging in barrel and time in the bottle.

[31] Kept in a dark wine cellar with 70 to 80% humidity at a temperature of roughly 13°C (55°F).

[32] While specific varieties of wine-making grapes have definite characteristics, much depends on the soil, climate, vintage and the influence of the winemaker.

33 While not Designated Regions, Prince Edward County (viticultural area) and Durham Region have shown that they can produce outstanding quality wine.

34 At the time of printing, a proposal was put forward to have the Niagara Peninsula broken down into 7 sub-appellations or regions. The breakdown of these regions will depend on climate, weather, soil and geographic location.

35 Wine matches by Chuck Byers.

36 This wine is produced by the Niagara College Teaching Winery and is a medium bodied blend of Marechal Foch, Gamay Noir and Baco Noir.

37 Made in the 'Traditional Method' or 'Methode Champenoise' whereby secondary fermentation takes place in the bottle—the same process used to make Champagne.

38 Made from berries obtained at Bumbleberry Orchards next to Fieldstone Winery in Alberta

39 Deboned.

40 Harley Hatfield was the fellow who lit the fuse that set off the dynamite that loosened the nails of the church discussed in the Blasted Church description. This is a V.Q.A. white varietal blend with a creamy texture. Check out the website.

41 Concerning sauces and wine matching: Wines are usually matched to the sauce, although consideration must be given to how the sauce is being used. Suggestions here are generic—without winery names.

42 Canned tomatoes are usually picked at the height of ripeness. Besides, who wants to peel tomatoes!

43 Tomatoes are seen as enemies of wine because of the preponderance of acid; however, a fruity/peppery wine such as a Merlot would balance the acid in a recipe.

44 Keep in mind that Shiraz is Syrah and Syrah is Shiraz.

45 Sauvignon Blanc has herbal and citrus qualities that would probably go better with the ingredients. The wine should also be unoaked so that the natural fruit flavours of the wine can be imparted to the ingredients.

46 This is the opposite to what the previous recipe suggested since here we need the roundness of an oaked Chardonnay with its complex creamy, vanilla, butterscotch and woody imparts to the recipe.

47 The 'heat' from the spices would overpower most wines. A cold beer is a solution.

48 **CAUTION: Whenever you add alcohol to a pan always remove the pan from the heat. Pour the alcohol away from you when adding to the pan. Covering the pan will prevent the alcohol from igniting. The lid can be removed once the sauce has slowly warmed to boiling.**

49 By turning the chicken over before placing in the oven, the egg mixture will seal the outside causing the chicken to steam and keep the chicken tender and juicy.

50 See section on sauces.

51 See section on sauces.

52 See the section on sauces regarding stir fry sauce.

[53] If beef or game is used in the stir-fry, use this wine or a similar red as part of the sauce.

[54] Submitted by Township Vineyards and Winery co-owner, Gwen Coleman.

[55] Known also as Weil Winery.

[56] Black Crowberry is a small round blackberry that grows close to the ground near Newfoundland's coastline. The technical name is Empetrum Nigrum and is also known as Blackberry, Foxberry and Crowberry to Newfoundlanders. High in anti-oxidants and nutrients, it was used for medicinal purposes decades ago. Technical information supplied by Winston Jennings, Weil Winery Nfld.

[57] Located in Prince Edward County near Picton.

[58] Located in Niagara-on-the-Lake.

[59] This is a Scottish Herbal Liqueur.

[60] Check out Greg Muscat's 'Ross Fil Forn' or Baked Rice Recipe as a side dish.

[61] Naked Grape Wines are located in Oliver, B.C., Niagara Falls, Ontario and Scoudouc, New Brunswick. They are a member of Vincor International.

[62] Roberto Fracchioni is the Executive Chef of the Millcroft Inn located in Alton, Ontario. He was formerly the Executive Chef of 'On The Twenty' at Cave Spring Cellars, Jordan.

[63] If a somewhat lighter wine is desired, try the Rossignol 'Selectionne Blanc'.

[64] Preferably a rich year like 2002.

[65] Alex is Head Chef at Le Caveau , at Grand Pre Vineyards, Nova Scotia.

[66] Located in Orford, Quebec.

[67] Located in Oshawa, Ontario.

[68] Demi-glace is the brown sauce that results by skimming the brown liquid in the pan, which is sometimes termed 'espagnole sauce'. The sauce can be made from boiling down the liquid to the desired consistency and/or by adding stock/meat juices to the liquid as it boils.

[69] Located in Whitby, Ontario and highlighted in the book 'Where to Eat in Canada'.

[70] A mixture of herbs such as rosemary, thyme, oregano, parsley, tarragon, chives and chervil.

[71] Chef Kevin and his 'Cooking Solutions' reside in Bear River, Nova Scotia.

[72] 2003 best of category, 'All Canadian Wine Championships'.

[73] Alta Rossa Restaurant is the best-kept secret in Toronto, Ontario. Consistently good, it offers four-star food at regular prices. It is located in Vaughan.

[74] Enotrium is the first of its kind in Ontario. Made similar to Amarone, the grapes are air dried for 20 to 30 days. Over 3 ½ lbs of grapes are used to make one bottle of Enotrium. The wine is a blend of Cabernet Sauvignon, Cabernet Franc and Merlot.

[75] Greg Muscat is a multi-talented artist with animal carving, photography, amateur cooking and toy making among his many pastimes.

[76] This is a traditional Maltese dish that was adapted by Greg Muscat for this book.

[77] Ier Cru or Premier Cru means 'First Growth' in French and has added meaning as the best of the best in Bordeaux communes.

78 Grenache is a grape variety indicative to southern and southwestern France and is used in the making of Vin Doux Naturels (reminiscent of Port) as well as Chateauneuf-du-Pape, general A.O.C. Rhone wines and Gigondas. It is also used in Spain, California and Australia.

79 Dennis Yurkiwsky mentions a note about cocoa mass in chocolate: “Cocoa mass is, not surprisingly, the mass of the cocoa bean. It consists of two components—the cocoa solids, as found in the cans and packages, and the cocoa butter, the oil from the cocoa bean. The average bean yields 53% butter and the balance in solids. The two are separated then recombined in the manufacture of the chocolate. When these two components are in balance, the higher % of cocoa mass in the chocolate, the flavour is more rich and intensive and the chocolate is smoother. When out of balance, the chocolate tends to be a bit bitter and the texture tends to feel grainy. Most definitely, the higher the cocoa mass, the lower the sugar. Popularly, one of the distinctions of each of the basic categories of chocolate was the % of cocoa mass (usually with the rather general descriptions of sweet, bittersweet, bitter and extra bitter). So that, fundamentally, one would choose their wine or beverage based upon the sweetness (% cocoa mass) of the chocolate.”

80 Magnotta and Southbrook make a great Framboise, made from raspberries (pour it over the ice-cream). Archibalds makes a great Iced Apple made from frozen apples.

81 Geisenheim/Seyval harvested in November in Quebec.

82 This section includes only the winery name, its winemaker and a description. For phone numbers and region, see the general winery list in this book. The wineries in this section are in Italics.

83 Vitis vinifera is the grape genus that such noble varieties of grapes as Cabernet Sauvignon, Merlot, Chardonnay and Pinot Noir belong to.

84 D’Angelo Estates Okanagan also has a Bed &Breakfast reviewed in another chapter.

85 Known as the “Royal Inniskilling Fusiliers”, check history at (www.regiments.org/regiments/uk/inf/027Innis.htm).

86 Marechal Foch is a vinifera hybrid. See also chapter titled ‘Canada Begins to Shine’ for further information on this event.

87 Vincor is was founded by Donald Triggs and Alan Jackson and now is considered the fourth largest wine related corporation in North America with holdings in Canada, United States, Australia, England and New Zealand. Donald Triggs is its CEO and President.

88 Tom Seaver and Kristine Casey are also responsible for the other wines made at Jackson-Triggs Niagara Estate Winery.

89 There are seven locations. Two of these (Vaughan and Beamsville) offer tours and educational tasting presentations.

90 Many of the unique names (such as Blasted Church, Therapy Vineyards, Dirty Laundry, Foofaraw Wines) come from the imaginative mind of Bernie Hadley-Beauregard of Brandever Strategy/Marketing Strategy + Design of Vancouver. See acknowledgements.

91 A French term that basically means the combined effects of the soil, weather, rain, sun, wind, geography and humans on the wine that is ultimately produced in a vineyard.

[92] Group Taillan is located in the Medoc Region of Bordeaux France and owns the following Chateaux: Gruaad-Larose, Ferriere, Haut-Bages Liberal, Chasse-Spleen, Citran, La Gurgue and it has the largest Appellation Controlee wines in France with vineyards in Bordeaux, Cotes du Rhone, Loire Valley, Provence and Languedoc.

[93] See Bed and Breakfast section under Windmill Bed and Breakfast.

[94] Little Sands is near Murray Harbour facing the Northumberland Strait and Nova Scotia.

[95] Presently there are seven acres of vineyards under cultivation at Rossignol Estates. Two of these are in greenhouses.

[96] A rare Russian variety of red grape used in making of some Nova Scotia wines.

[97] An early developing Russian grape used in the making of some Nova Scotia wines.

[98] Also known as Notre Dame Wines.

[99] See Bed and Breakfast section for description of the island's history.

[100] Opened in 2005.

[101] New winery being established for 2007. Owners Gerry McConnell and Dara Gordon. Outstandingly beautiful vineyards just a stone's throw from Gaspereau Vineyards.

[102] Blomindon is owned by Creekside Winery in Jordan, Ontario, excellent potential and scenic location.

[103] Owned by Jost Vineyards, Malagash, North Shore Nova Scotia.

[104] Winemaker Bruce Ewert (BSc. Bio-Resource Engineering, 18 years wine making experience. To open in 2008.

[105] First true commercial grape winery in New Brunswick.

[106] Very close to American border, it is said that border runs through local Opera House. Is located very high up in hills with panoramic view of Vermont.

[107] The Dunham microclimate allows for some hardier Vitis vinifera to be grown.

[108] Name means 'Boar's Den' in English.

[109] Organic winery.

[110] Almost spanking new. Great promise.

[111] Farmed by religious order dating back to early 18th century.

[112] Old mill dating to 1695 is located here.

[113] Creekside has a partnership with the Mike Weir Winery.

[114] Same owners as Niagara Cellars and Thomas & Vaughan Estates.

[115] Originally owned by Andres.

[116] One of the original Sunnieholme wineries built in 1918.

[117] Also same owners as Vinoteca in Woodbridge.

[118] Owned by Niagara Cellars who also own Maple Grove Winery.

[119] At the time of printing this book, there are several new wineries that will open shortly (2005-2006) in Southwestern Ontario including Lake Erie North Shore: Aleksander Estate Winery,

Mastronardi Estate Winery, Muscedere Vineyards, Smith & Wilson Estate Winery, Sprucewood Shores and Colchester Ridge.

[120] Canada's most southern winery.

[121] Also known as degree-days, this is a term that describes the climatic potential of a district. The temperature values (above 50°F or 10°C) are computed daily during the growing season (April to October). The total gives a value that represents the potential for a district. There is little growth under the minimum temperature of 50°F or 10°C.

[122] Presently sold through Black Prince Vineyards—winery and tasting room being built.

[123] Owned by wine writer and columnist Dick Singer and son, Steven. First trial vintage planned for fall 2005.

[124] Advertised as Ontario's first Apple Fruit Winery.

[125] Winner of 3 Bronze Medals at 2003 Canadian Wine Awards and Silver at 2004 All Canadian Wine Competition.

[126] Rigby Black Currant fruit wines are shipped to Roaming River Ranches in Alberta.

[127] Lotusland was known as A'very Fine Winery but went through a name change some 2 years ago. The 'A'very' name is now used as a brand name due to popular demand.

[128] Family wine making goes back to 17th century France.

[129] In 2004, Cherrypoint was purchased from owners, Wayne and Helena Ulrich, by the Cowichan Tribe making them the 2nd First Nations group to get involved in vineyard ownership and winemaking.

[130] Winery is on an actual island, the second largest in the group.

[131] Township 7 opened in Langley, B.C. in 2001 and now has opened a winery in the Naramata Bench.

[132] Honey Wine. Tugwell is B.C.'s first Meadery.

[133] Church and State Wines is the new name for the Victoria Estate Winery and is planning to reopen sometime in 2005-6. Burrowing Owl's former winemaker, Bill Dyers has now taken over the reins at Church and State.

[134] The only desert region in Canada with less than 6 inches of rain per year.

[135] Located in Cache Creek.

[136] Benchlands is sister winery to Mistral Estates Winery and Spiller Estates Winery and B&B (see listings).

[137] Located in the Kootenays within the Colombia River Valley.

[138] Formerly Scherzinger Vineyards Cottage Winery.

[139] Phone number not available. Try contacting Brandever Strategy Inc. (604) 269-2326.

[140] See Benchland Vinyards, Spillers Estates.

[141] Jackson-Triggs Winery number.

[142] World's only winery specializing in icewines.

[143] Part of Hawthorne Mountain Wines.

[144] See Benchland Vineyards, Mistral Estate .

[145] New Winery, check with Brandever Strategy Inc., (604) 269-2326.

[146] While the utmost care has been taken in selecting these Bed and Breakfasts, most contacts were made via email and websites on the Internet. They have been selected for their proximity to wine regions/wineries. The authors always encourage visitors to research any place that they intend to stay prior to making reservations or any such plans.

[147] Gorgeous Vineyards, which are due to open around 2007 but whose beauty can be appreciated, now.

[148] To go to Indian Point website go to the New Brunswick website listed and click the site map and then click accommodations. Click the Port Elgin area that will take you to the Indian Point website.

[149] Barbecues are seasonal in the summer.

[150] Designated a Five Star Resort by Canada Select.

[151] Named for Col. James S. King.

[152] The Bostwick House was the home of the founder of Port Stanley (where the Telegraph House is located), Colonel Bostwick.

[153] Pelee Passage.

[154] Vin Villa is the remains of Canada's first commercial winery at Lighthouse and Fish Points.

[155] Fish Point, Lighthouse Point, Glacial Grooves to name a few areas.

[156] Bird Migration, Monarch Butterfly Migration, Bald Eagles, Wolves, etc.

[157] Fishing licenses must be obtained.

[158] See description in Winery Section.

[159]www.peleeisland.com

Printed in the United States
50441LVS00002B/1-102

9 781897 160183